Rabbits For Prizes And Profit...

Charles Rayson

Nabu Public Domain Reprints:

You are holding a reproduction of an original work published before 1923 that is in the public domain in the United States of America, and possibly other countries. You may freely copy and distribute this work as no entity (individual or corporate) has a copyright on the body of the work. This book may contain prior copyright references, and library stamps (as most of these works were scanned from library copies). These have been scanned and retained as part of the historical artifact.

This book may have occasional imperfections such as missing or blurred pages, poor pictures, errant marks, etc. that were either part of the original artifact, or were introduced by the scanning process. We believe this work is culturally important, and despite the imperfections, have elected to bring it back into print as part of our continuing commitment to the preservation of printed works worldwide. We appreciate your understanding of the imperfections in the preservation process, and hope you enjoy this valuable book.

Rabbits For Prizes and Profit.

PART I.

GENERAL MANAGEMENT.
PART I.

By CHARLES RAYSON.

ILLUSTRATED.

LONDON:
"THE BAZAAR" OFFICE, 32, WELLINGTON-STREET,
STRAND, W.C.

PRICE SIXPENCE.

ADVERTISEMENTS.

NET MAKERS TO HER MAJESTY THE QUEEN.

NEW GARDEN NETS, TENTS, MARQUEES, and RICK CLOTHS.

A good Second-hand Garden Net, 4yds. wide, 28s., 2yds. 14s., the 100yds. run; large size Purse Nets, 7s. per dozen; large size Gamekeepers' Capes, lined, 12s. 6d., unlined, 7s. 6d.

Rabbit Nets, corded ready for use, for shooting or catching.

Hay Cloths, Tarpaulins, and Cart Covers; also, Bird, Pheasant, Poultry, and Fishing Nets of every description.

J. ALLEN and SON, Manufacturers,
11, SEYMOUR-STREET, EUSTON-ROAD, LONDON, N.W.

RABBITS.

MESSRS. THOS. C. and H. LORD have, during the greater part of the Season, a number of Rabbits surplus over those they keep for Exhibition, which they are willing to sell at moderate prices. The stock includes Lops, Silver Greys, Himalayans, Angoras, and Dutch, many of them prize winners, and fit for exhibition—same strain as their noted "Champions," which have won so many Silver Cups, Medals, and other Prizes at the principal Shows throughout the Kingdom.

MR. A. H. EASTEN, of Rutland Villa, Botanic-lane, Hull, has continually Surplus Stock from his celebrated LOP-EARED, HIMALAYA, and other RABBITS, of prize strains, which he will sell at reasonable rates, according to age.—Prices and full particulars on application.

LOP-EARED RABBITS.

MR. E. FROST, of Hackbridge, Carshalton, Surrey, has generally a quantity of these RABBITS for disposal. They are from the best prize-winning strains in the country. The price varies according to age, length of ear, &c.—Full particulars will be forwarded on receipt of letter.

FANCY PRIZE RABBITS, of every variety kept in this country, from my well-known Stock (which I keep for amusement), of which at times I have more than I care to have, and shall be glad to spare a few specimens to those desirous of improving their Stock.—CHARLES RAYSON, Esq., Ivy Lodge, Sidsbury, near Manchester.

WM. WHITWORTH, Jun., 30, Birch-lane, Longsight, Manchester, will have some Young Ones to SELL, from all his PRIZE RABBITS (Angora, Himalayan, Patagonian or Andalusian, Belgian Hare, and Dutch), at prices according to quality and age.

SECOND EDITION. Large post 8vo., price 6d.

BREEDING POULTRY FOR PRIZES—Being full directions for the proper selection of stock birds, the points required, &c., for the successful production of prize poultry, and numerous first-class wood engravings of fowls and feathers, showing the shapes and markings that must be aimed at. By JAMES LONG (winner of the New York Poultry Society's Prize for the best "Thesis on the Breeding and Management of Poultry").

Large post 8vo., price 6d.

EXHIBITION POULTRY (Part I.)—Being minute and accurate descriptions of Cochins, Dorkings, Spanish, Brahmas, French Fowl, Game, and their varieties, such as they must be to entitle them to success in the show pen. By JAMES LONG. Illustrated with four full-page portraits of prize birds.

Large post 8vo., price 6d.

EXHIBITION POULTRY (Part II.)—Being minute and accurate descriptions of Hamburghs, Polands, Malays, Bantams, "Any other Varieties," and Turkeys, such as they must be to entitle them to success in the show pen. By JAMES LONG. Illustrated with four full-page portraits of prize winners.

"THE BAZAAR" OFFICE, 32, WELLINGTON STREET, LONDON, W.C.

THE ANGORA RABBIT.

Rabbits For Prizes and Profit.

PART I.

GENERAL MANAGEMENT.

INTRODUCTION.

A LEARNED philosopher once said that he scarce thought it possible to find a man of any worth in the varied walks of life who had not his "hobby" of some kind; and it will be my task in the present work to furnish as much information as I can on one of the most widely spread. A great deal may have been said respecting rabbits, and many books written as guides to those anxious to rear these beautiful and interesting creatures; yet, in this age of exhibitions, and when perhaps more interest is felt, and we hear more of them than hitherto, it may not be deemed a work of supererogation to say further respecting our favourites. The fancy rabbits are undoubtedly of foreign origin; and from reliable information I should incline to the belief that Persia was the original home of, at least, some of the varieties, and I rather think that India and China may also have been the countries from which several of our distinct varieties have come. That rabbits are more cared for now, as "pets," than, say twenty, or even a dozen years ago, is very evident from the number we find exhibited, the interest they afford, and the importance committees attach to them at the various shows. Rabbits kept for amusement and for exhibition we may consider as a "hobby;" when kept for the former reason it is for the love of keeping them, and when for the second for love, profit, and honour combined, inasmuch as the prizes received are of value, and also stamp the taker's stock as valuable. Fancy rabbits are not, perhaps, so easily reared as their less valuable companions, the common ones, yet, with care and study of their requirements, they are by no means difficult to manage with success. My own experience, which is that of many years, as a breeder of every known variety of fancy hutch-rabbits, convinces me that to commence with the expensive "fancy" kinds causes an inexperienced breeder to suffer great disappointment, and often discourages him from afterwards attempting the rearing of the most valuable of the "fancy" varieties. He should procure some strong and less costly specimen, upon which his inexperience is to be practised, and in the event of failure, or loss of a few of them by accident, improper feeding or housing, such loss will be, in a commercial point of view, less grievous than with more costly ones. The grey, or grey and white, also black and white, as regards colour, may be bought for about three or four shillings a couple at six months old, and from these may be gained experience, and if they are not paired too soon—not until nine or ten months old, to insure strength and arrival at maturity—valuable lessons may be learnt of immense use in the future, when the knowledge is required for a variety as valuable in pounds as the previous ones were in shillings. For the selecting of healthy rabbits, care should be taken to obtain those with claws small, and not beyond the fur of the foot, as this is proof that they are young. When the claws are long and thick you may be assured the animals are aged; the claws of an old rabbit, of, say four or more years, are generally curved, and at times over an inch beyond the fur, and proportionate in thickness. The teeth of a young rabbit are small as compared with the older ones. Let the eye be full and sparkling, and the white portion free from that yellow tinge so indicative of ill health, and the body not swollen or with "pot-belly," which is a proof of feeding upon too much wet green food. The bowels of healthy rabbits are in a satisfactory state when the dung is in round balls, and a general sprightly vivacious manner seems always to be evident when the animal is in good health. A young fancier may commence, say with three does and one buck, taking care that they are not related, in order to insure healthy litters; and if he has room enough, and wishes to become an extensive breeder at once, six or eight does will not be too many for one buck, but, as before stated, the animals must be fully grown and kept warm.

CHAPTER I.

HUTCHES.

As to the kind of hutches, a great and learned man once said, "Any man can make a rabbit hutch." This I rather question, in the same manner as I should an assertion that a man who can cause the strings of a violin to vibrate is a player. Hutches are of great importance, especially if rabbits are valuable, and of pure and the more delicate breeds; and it is a mistake to suppose that any tub full of holes for a superabundant ventilation, will do for a rabbit hutch, the more especially if it is to be exposed to the weather as what may be called an "outside hutch." Any building, as a stable or unoccupied outbuilding, of dimensions, say from 4yds. square, and of brickwork and lofty, 9ft. and upwards, with good ventilation, will do well as a rabbitry. It should be fitted up on three sides with hutches in stacks, three or four in height, with the first floor 9in. from the ground, and 20in. from back to front, or 24in. for the larger varieties, as Patagonian lops or Belgian hares. It would not be requisite to have backs to the hutches if these are placed close to the wall, which should be a thick and dry one, but if otherwise, a ½in. back would be requisite to insure protection from damp, as that is of vast importance. The second and other floors should be 18in. above one another, and made of ¾in. white deal, and each floor should be 1½in. lower at the back than the front, and the back edge should be provided with a zinc gutter, 1½in. across, to carry off the urine into a pail placed for the purpose at the end of the hutch. But rabbits, if properly fed upon dry food, which is undoubtedly the safest, do not make their hutches so damp as might be supposed. I have seen large rabbitries, with nearly one hundred rabbits in them, in some thirty hutches, and all the floors were perfectly level from back to front, but, nevertheless, I consider that the floor on an incline is preferable to the other. Three tiers of hutches, the height given, and 9in. from the ground or floor, will give, including the thickness of floors, a full height of some 5ft. 6in., quite high enough for convenience of seeing the rabbits, or cleaning. If one floor be 14in.

in height for the smaller varieties, as Dutch or Himalayan, that would lower the total height, and even a little lower would do for the young rabbits just removed from the doe, yet, as a general rule, the more lofty the better to insure health. The length of hutch for larger rabbits should be 4ft. 6in., of which 1ft. 3in. should be set apart as a dark or sleeping room, the division being made with a loose or sliding partition, having an arched hole large enough for entrance, taking care that the edges of this entrance are rounded and smooth, so as not to injure the fur, and edged with thin zinc to prevent gnawing; thin zinc should also be tacked upon the edges of all woodwork liable to be injured by the teeth, as for instance the little fender, which is some 2in. deep, and used in front of each hutch to keep in the bedding. When young rabbits are in the higher hutches, a small light frame of $\frac{1}{2}$in. wood and 8in. high, and covered with wire netting of 1in. mesh, fixing into the floor with iron pins, is of great use for preventing them falling down, for they will clamour at the door at the approach of anyone, especially at feeding time, and the want of such protection results in too many instances of injury and broken legs. The outward appearance of the hutches may be made as ornamental as taste and financial resources will allow. Polished mahogany doors, and white or brass handles I have at times seen, and they add to the neatness; yet a less costly exterior, combined with neat design and convenience, looks well.

If the rabbits are in "outside hutches," care should be taken to give them a south aspect if possible, and shutters for use in the winter weather should be provided; and ventilation, which should always be *above* the head of the rabbit, should not be forgotten. The roof should be well slated and pointed, as warmth is of great importance, and perfect protection from cold winds must be provided. The strong perpendicular wire, when set only $\frac{3}{8}$in. apart, is undoubtedly the best protection from vermin, though it does not allow the rabbits to be seen to the same advantage as when the hexagon 1in. wire netting is used. This latter should be strong or it is liable to be torn down by the teeth and feet, especially by the larger varieties of rabbits. The hutch for a single buck requires no division, and need only be 2ft. 9in. long, by 2ft. wide, according to the space at disposal, and for the breeding does the sizes given above may be reduced if requisite, in order to increase the number of hutches, yet rabbits should not be in too confined a space, or their health will suffer. A small hutch, of course, will do for the young rabbits, and requires no division. I would not advise too many in one hutch—about twelve—and these, until four months old, would do well in the same size of hutch as given for the does. Of course the size and shape of hutch must depend upon taste and space at disposal, and each fancier is generally best able to give his ideas to the carpenter.

If the question of cost is not a consideration, the double-floored hutch is probably the best in every respect; yet, as rabbits

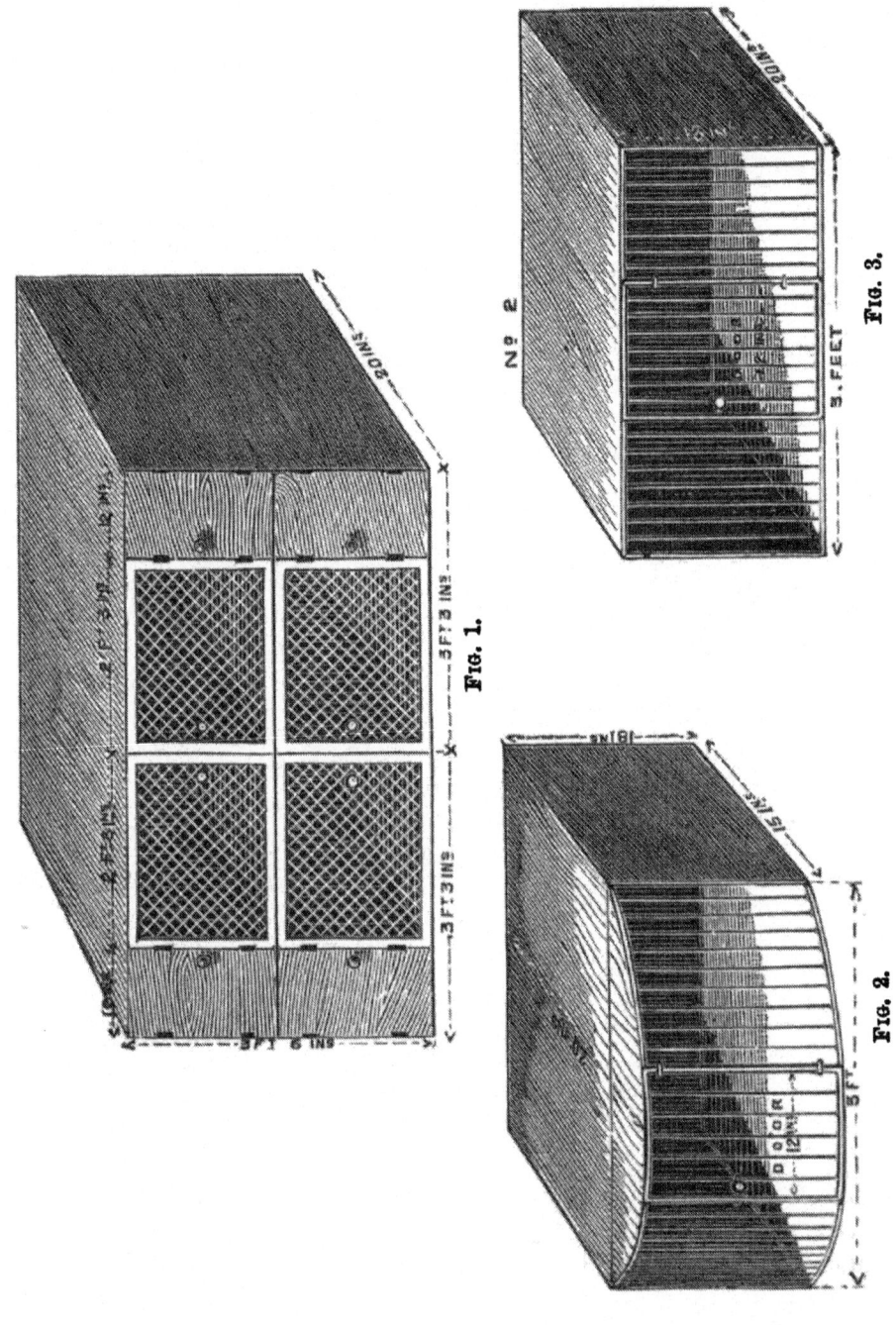

are kept by fanciers in almost every position in life, it is wise perhaps to suggest such as may be brought within the reach of all, from the cheapest to the most costly and ornamental, though not forgetting the real points of excellence—viz., convenience and the healthiness of the inmates.

Perhaps one of the most perfect hutches that could be found, particularly for sweetness, &c., is the one with the double floor. The bottom floor, which may be made of pine ¾in. or 1in. thick, and inclined towards the back, as noticed before, can then be covered with zinc, tacked down, and above that the upper floor made of laths, ½in. thick, 1in. apart, placed in any position—at right angles, or diagonally—leaving the 1in. hole for all droppings to pass through to the zinc floor below (see Fig. 4), to be swept and washed away into the receptacle at the back, leaving all as clean as possible. It is better to round the upper edges of the laths, as it facilitates the litter passing through, and does not allow of wet remaining upon the surface. If these laths are of the size given, they will be quite strong enough when so close together, and if put together in two or three pieces or frames, they will perhaps be more convenient for removing when requisite, which will be seldom, as this lattice work can be occasionally washed as it remains, and will soon dry ready for the straw bed. This upper floor should be 1½in. from the other, resting upon pieces of wood at each end of the hutch, and if a long one, a centre piece as support might be added to insure firmness. Another kind of upper floor I have tried for small hutches is made of strong ¾in. mesh galvanized wire, but as it was more elastic than the wood, it was not quite so satisfactory, though it was easily cleaned with the brush. Another kind of floor for a hutch at times found useful is a slate slab ½in. thick. It can be as easily cleaned as the zinc, but requires great strength of framework to support it, and cannot so conveniently be used for the portable hutch in consequence of its weight, but for fixed hutches in "stacks" it answers tolerably well. These last described are the most expensive and complete hutches. The great consideration unquestionably is the convenience of size, general arrangement, suitability to the requirements of the occupants, and perfect security from cold. The illustrations given, as will be observed, are from the most simple box-like hutches, procurable by the juvenile fancier, to the more costly ones found in the rabbitry of the more fortunate owner of choice and costly specimens of our fancy favourites.

Fig. 1 is for breeding does and very young rabbits, as it contains dark or sleeping compartments. These compartments are 12in. wide, and the depth and height of the hutch.

Figs. 2 and 3 need no explanation.

Fig. 4 represents a stack of eight hutches 3ft. across the front of each, 2ft. deep, and 18in. high, and of use for a single rabbit, or two or three half-grown ones. A separate door may be given to each hutch, or one door full height of 3ft. will do. It will be noticed that the hutches at the bottom left hand and bottom right hand corners have the lattice-work floors of wood or wire.

One of my correspondents, a practical fancier says. "I do not approve of No. 1 hutch for breeding, as it does not contain the sliding partition: and then again a double hutch cannot be kept as clean and sweet as a single one, inasmuch as the urine from the top compartment is liable to get through in some cases, and fall on to the rabbit which lives in the bottom one, which is injurious to the health. By the word 'double-hutch' I do not mean one with false floor, but one with two compartments in one hutch, the one above the other. I do not approve of zinc floors, except where there is a false floor above, for the following reason: To breed

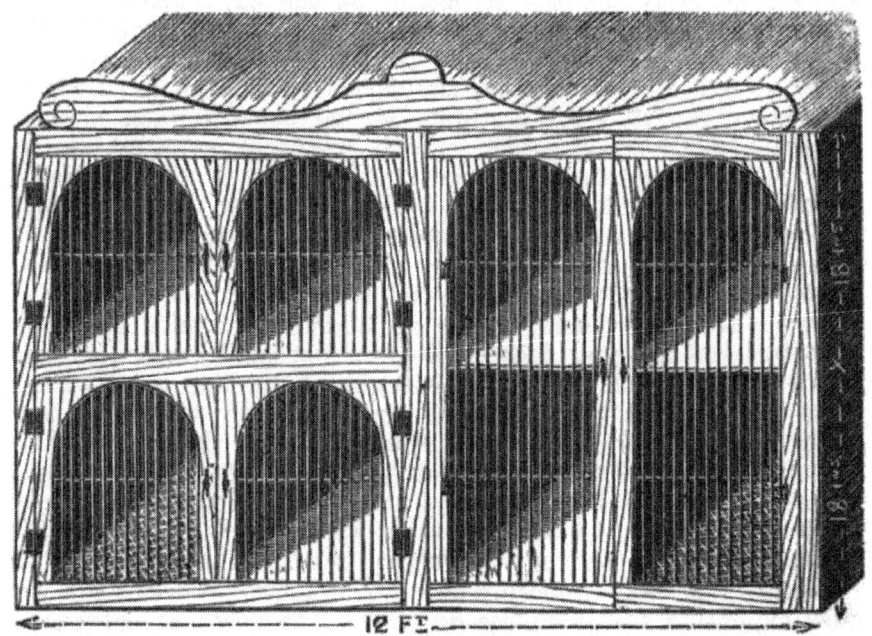

FIG. 4. STACK OF HUTCHES.

rabbits properly they *must* be kept at one uniform heat till fully developed. Now on a zinc floor the rabbit's feet are much colder than on a lattice or wooden floor, therefore in the winter time the zinc keeps the hutch cool just when it ought to be warm." Mr. T. C. Lord, of Huddersfield, says: "As regards the formation of hutches there is only a slight difference in those recommended by Mr. Rayson and those I use in my rabbit houses, and that difference is in the one used for breeding purposes. The hutch represented in the illustration (Fig. 5), is about 4ft. in length, 2ft. in width, and the same in height. It contains a false floor, which, by the way, is constructed rather differently from those mentioned by Mr. Rayson; it also contains a sliding partition for the sleeping or breeding compartment, and a drawer underneath the false floor to contain the dung, urine, spent litter, &c. This drawer is an addition I have not seen in any hutch except my own; but it is a very valuable addition. A. is the false floor, which is constructed as follows: a framework is made of wood about 1½in. thick, this framework to fit into the open compartment, but not into the breeding compartment; on to this framework is fixed a number of laths about ½in. thick, and ½in. apart, not a full inch as stated by Mr. Rayson, for the reason that—when the laths are placed too far apart, the young rabbits are apt to get their feet through, and in some instances break their legs. These laths are fixed on to the framework straight across, somewhat after the style of a joist, so that they do not project beyond the edges of the frame-work. This mode of false floor answers better than one made with laths fixed in squares or diagonals, inasmuch as the dung, &c., has a better chance of falling through the spaces. The sliding partition (B) requires no explanation as the illustration speaks for itself. The drawer (C) is made like an ordinary drawer, and is lined with tin

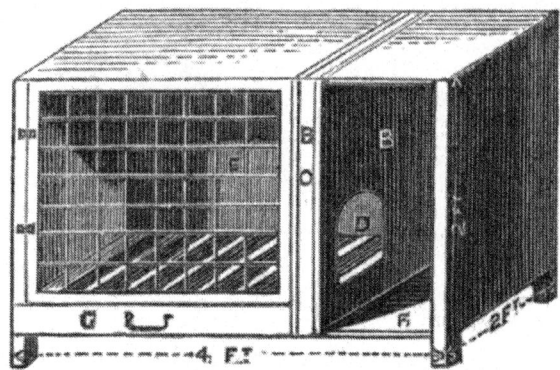

FIG. 5. BREEDING HUTCH COMPLETE.

A, False Floor; BB, Sliding partition; C, Drawer; D, Hole leading to breeding box; E, Wire front, to open as a door; F, Breeding compartment.

or zinc. The use of this drawer is to catch the droppings from the false floor, and for the better convenience in cleaning, as it only requires drawing out and emptying, and cleansing with water, and saves the trouble of taking out the false floor. Where there are several hutches of this kind, which is only in isolated cases, such as where the fancier keeps a large stock, it is a good plan to have an extra drawer to put in the hutch whilst one of the others is being cleaned out, and then none of the droppings can fall into the bottom of the hutch itself."

Mr. T. C. Lord further describes a breeding hutch, which he strongly recommends, especially for lops, for which he is so well known: "An illustration is here given of a hutch which is used exclusively for the breeding and rearing of lop-eared rabbits. The success to be attained from the use of this hutch is obvious, when it can be truthfully stated that most of the prize lop-eared rabbits now exhibited at the poultry and rabbit shows are bred in hutches made on a similar plan to the one given in the engraving. This kind of hutch is not now generally known to the majority of rabbit fanciers, as the success attained from its use has made a few of our breeders rather dubious at letting others into the 'secret.' It is used by many of the successful breeders and exhibitors at our principal 'Rabbit Clubs' throughout the kingdom.

"It is a well known fact that the secret of obtaining length of ears in lops is by employing heat, and this hutch is so constructed as to cause greater attraction of the heat to the inside of it, and thus produce the desired effect. The rabbitry in which this hutch is used should be kept at a constant heat of not less than sixty or seventy degrees during the time of breeding and bringing up. The rabbitry may be kept at the above-mentioned heat by using one of either of the following stoves, viz., Bamford's patent hot air stove, or Walker's patent self-feeder; either of these may be obtained from any respectable ironmonger's. These stoves may be

FIG. 5A. BREEDING HUTCH FOR LOPS.

A. Door to general living compartment; B². Glass in front of door to attract heat; C. Sliding partition into breeding box; D. Top door to breeding box; E. Bottom ditto; F. Side rest for glass to slide down.

regulated to keep burning from five to ten hours, according to the heat required, with only once feeding. During the whole of the winter of 1871-72 I had one of the former stoves in my own rabbitry (which is about thirty feet long by ten feet wide, and is built of wood, with glass skylights), and found it to answer better than any other I have tried, as by feeding it about ten o'clock at night I could leave it with safety and find it still burning in the morning. It is fed from the top with coke broken up into small pieces, and may be kept at any degree of heat by means of a regulator at the bottom. I have heard of some few breeders who have their rabbitries heated at as much as eighty, and in one or two cases ninety degrees; but this, I consider, is going to extremes, and more likely to do injury than good, as the rabbits are so overpowered by the excessive heat when young, that they never gain the size so desirable in lop-eared rabbits, and which can be obtained by the more moderate use of heat. Another reason to be taken into consideration against excessive heat is that when the rabbits are sent out to any of the shows for exhibition they are always liable to catch cold, more especially during cold weather, and when the show extends over one day, and the rabbits have to remain out on the show field, or in a room at a low temperature, all night; in fact, it has occurred in some cases that rabbits have died in a few days after reaching home, and the only reason to be assigned as to the cause of their death is that they have caught a severe cold when away from home.

"The illustration, Fig. 5A, gives a perspective view of the hutch named, but as its construction throughout perhaps may not be clearly understood from the engraving by some of my readers, I will give a minute description of its various parts. The door to the general living compartment (A) is made to cover the greater part of the hutch, and has an open space in the centre about twelve inches square (B), with wires fixed in it. At each side of the space is fastened a piece of wood (F), with a groove cut in the inner edge for the glass B^2 to slide down in a slanting position as shown in the engraving. This glass is the cause of the greater attraction of the heat to the inside of the hutch, and by this means keeping the rabbits at a higher temperature, and causing their ears to grow both quicker and longer. The sliding partition (C) is made on the same principle as the one described in my former hutch. The door to the breeding compartment, which opens from the outside, is in my own breeding hutches made rather differently from any I have yet seen, and is, I consider, an improvement on the old style. It is made in two parts, the top part (D) being made to open separately from the other, so that the breeder may examine the young rabbits just after the doe has kindled, and select those which he intends to let the doe rear, and by leaving the bottom door (E) closed, the nest is not so liable to get disturbed, or any of the young ones fall out, which is frequently the case in hutches with one door only. This hutch may either have the false floor and drawer mentioned in my previous article, or be left without, as the breeder chooses. No ventilation holes are required, as a sufficiency of air will get into the hutch through the wire opening in front of the larger door.

"As an example of the success obtained from the use of this hutch, I may state that the yellow and white doe with ears 23in. long, which won so many prizes for myself and brother during the season of 1872, as well as many others of our prize winners, all with ears measuring over 22 inches, were bred in a hutch similar in almost every respect to the one described above."

CHAPTER II.

BREEDING.

I SHALL presume that the rabbits are just the kind desired, and may here state that the judicious purchase of a breeding stock is most important for many reasons. I strongly advise the selection of young rabbits, from four to six months old, as they are then more safe, having passed through the first moults, which are at times so fatal to them; and if the cost is proportionately more by reason of their age, yet it must not be forgotten that a certain amount of safety may reasonably be expected as an equivalent.

I do not advocate the pairing of rabbits too young, especially if they are valuable, and the young are intended to be reared. I have tried all ages from six months, and decidedly prefer the ages of ten or twelve months, for when fully grown, or nearly so, they have greater strength, and this I think eventually pays, for you gain in quality what may seem to have been lost in number, by not having had litters when the does were two or three months younger. Respecting the selecting the best specimen of each kind to rear the future stock from, I shall, when describing each variety and their peculiarities, speak more fully; yet this much must be said, that the more perfect and healthy the pair are, the greater the certainty of valuable litters, and yet to this rule there are exceptions.

The buck and doe should not be in the same hutch many minutes together, and for pairing the months of February or March are the best to insure healthy stock; yet, when rabbits are kept in warm comfortable hutches, they *may* litter at any time during the year, but, as before said, this should not be allowed; four litters during the twelve months are ample. If any longer time is allowed between any litter than three months, it should be during the coldest weather, when to give the does, (especially older ones) a little extra rest may prove an advantage. During the inclement weather of January, extra care and warmth and feeding must not be forgotten, and any little attention more than requisite during the warmer weather will be more than compensated for by the health and satisfactory appearance of both mother and offspring. When within a few days of the time for littering, the doe will, if of the right sort, furnish sufficient evidence of the fact by biting the straw into short pieces, and carrying it and the hay, of which she should have abundance, in her mouth to some favourite corner of the hutch; and here I may state that the hutch should be at this time well cleaned and disinfected, for this will be the last thorough cleansing it can have for a short time, in consequence of its delicate occupants. The hutch should be dry and placed upon the floor, if not constructed upon the double floor plan referred to in my remarks upon hutches. The precise day will be known by reference to the list of does, kept in a book, with the dates of their visiting the buck. In addition I recommend the plan of labels of wood or slate, 2½in. long by 2½in. broad, fixed to the wire of each hutch, and bearing dates corresponding to those in the book alluded to. The book should also give the number brought forth at each litter, and thus is valuable as showing the yearly total produced by each doe; the label can be easily cleaned and prepared for other dates. I find this plan by far the best, and least trouble, as by it you can at once see what event may be expected, and when. When the thirty days of gestation have expired (or even the day before), the doe should have a little clean water to drink, in a separate dish to her ordinary one for feeding from. An intense thirst is at times experienced at this critical time, and to possess the means of relief is often to save the progeny. Care should also be taken that the hutch is mouse proof, for it is astonishing what a serious result these little pests cause at times to the more timid does, who are very likely, on the presence of these intruders, to either neglect their young or even devour them, as though they thought they would thus prevent the mice destroying them. It is astonishing how easily some does are startled, especially those of a nervous temperament.

A sudden clap of thunder will at times cause the does to miscarry, and their litters may be found scattered about in various parts of the hutch; and such a premature birth is to lose them all. I may here state that all strangers, when visiting the rabbitry, should do so quietly, as a sudden rush into the presence of the rabbits is sure to startle, and probably produce injurious results amongst the pregnant does. All strange dogs should be excluded. Avoid at all times touching the nest or the young, for some does are very suspicious, and strongly object to any interference with their domestic and family arrangements, and I have sometimes noticed their anxious eyes following my hand when attempting to touch their offspring. In this particular does are very different, and I have had some seemingly quite confident that no harm will befall their young; yet, it is far better to leave them untouched, for the cold hand will almost be sure to chill the newly-born rabbit. Should any die at this early stage of their existence the doe will soon remove them, generally placing them near the door of her hutch. Some few young does will throw their young ones about the hutch soon after they are born, and then seem to take no further notice of them, but there is generally a cause, as mice running across the nest, or some dog or cat presenting themselves in front of the hutch. Such does may be tried again, and when about to litter supplied with a little water, and a clean well-ventilated hutch with a darker portion for the nest. Try to find out the cause, and if there is not any, the doe may be considered unfit for keeping for breeding purposes. At times a change of hutch insures success.

Suckling does should have a liberal supply of warm milk and bread; I rarely resort to any other material for the morning and evening feeds than this nutritious "first course," which generally brings both mother and family through the first three weeks satisfactorily; but a supply of carrots, swedes, oats, boiled Indian meal, in form of a paste, are also requisite at this time. Avoid any aqueous food likely to disarrange the bowels; a few soaked peas will tend to restore the doe to her original strength. When milk and bread are used for does just littering, a separate dish for this purpose is better than the ordinary one, for whilst that for the dry food is easily kept sweet and clean, the dish for milk is liable to become sour, especially in warm weather, and it should therefore be washed or scalded every day, for the does have a strong objection to the unpalatable smell, and give evidence of this by refusing to eat their food at times. Between the fifteenth and eighteenth day from birth the young rabbits may be seen peeping out from their nest, which in a few days more may be removed, and the hutch undergo a thorough cleaning. If another well-ventilated hutch is ready to receive them, equally warm, all the better—and here I may say that a few spare hutches are always useful for this purpose, in order to allow recently occupied ones to have time for ventilation, and again be made ready for use. If, say in a stock of some twenty-five does, one third of them have litters at the same date, the same warm food and general feeding spoken of will be found advantageous; and the spare hutches should be in process of preparation for the convalescents. Another advantage in some eight or ten does littering about the same date, is, that should any of them be burdened with a too large family, one or two may be transferred to another hutch, where the occupants in the nest are not so numerous. If it is at all requisite to do this, the sooner it is done after birth the better, as before the fur commences to grow the foster-mother will be less liable to discover the presence of strangers with her own family. A doe may also give evidence of debility, and so the rearing of two or three less will tend to her restoration to original strength. If any "nurses" should be found requisite, the little Dutch are as valuable as any for the purpose, as they are of a kind disposition, have generally abundance of milk, and are strong and hardy. As a general rule each doe will bring up her own litters the best. I have tried all sorts of experiments in this particular, and have arrived at this conclusion. At times only one or two of the most promising in the litters are left with the doe, in order that they may be larger, and more fit for exhibition or stock purposes.

When the young rabbits begin to leave their nest, they soon commence to feed with the mother, and acquire considerable confidence, as though they were quite safe in presenting themselves round the feeding dish. When the young rabbits are six or eight weeks old they may be removed from the doe; one or two of the stronger ones each day is perhaps the best plan, as this gradual removal seems better to dry up any milk she may have; and when all her family are removed from her care, a little salt in her beans or oats will be beneficial, as it tends to entirely dry up any milk that may be left, and, with good feeding, she may in ten days, again visit the buck, yet an extra few days of delay is at times an advantage to a doe which has brought up a large litter. The young rabbits may be allowed to run together until four months old, as a rule, with safety, but after that age they should be separated, for they are rather pugnacious, especially the bucks, and require a hutch for each sex, and even then with each other they are not always of the most peaceful disposition, and in a few weeks it is generally found the safest method to give each buck a hutch to himself, for their remaining together is often to allow them to injure each other, and totally destroy their usefulness for stock purposes. The does are less quarrelsome, and frequently some half dozen of them may be kept together until selected for pairing.

The young rabbits, when some eight or ten weeks old, pass through a moult, which is a critical time, and they require a little extra care in consequence; after that period is over they are more safe, and there is a probability that they will thrive with the requisite care. They should have a liberal supply of crushed oats for the first few weeks, at least; carrots, turnips, &c., will be safe diet; sweet hay, plenty of fresh (not cold) air; and this last is highly important, as no doubt a great proportion of the deaths of young rabbits before six months old have been caused by want of this and of cleanliness, and due care as to the right kind of food given; for this is generally the point where the error is committed—young rabbits being more frequently seen suffering from the effects of injurious food than from the want of a sufficiency of the right kind. Only a very small percentage of the rabbits should be lost, except from an epidemic or a series of accidents. Young rabbits, it will be found, consume a great deal more food than the matured ones in proportion to their size, and although they are constantly eating, they will not injure themselves, and not many of the "pot-bellied" kind will be found in the rabbitry if the food is good. The quantity to be given to half-a-dozen ten or twelve-week-old rabbits, will soon be ascertained. They are very fond of scratching their food out of the dish, which should therefore be so constructed as to prevent such waste. A very good description of trough for this purpose will be found in the next chapter. If these general rules are observed, but a small percentage of rabbits born will die from disease.

CHAPTER III.

FEEDING.

Give a bed of oat straw, as it seems to the rabbits sweeter and softer than the wheat or other kinds, and, if they eat it freely, always take care that it is dry and free from any mouldy smell, which is very offensive to the rabbits. To this add, as a feed during the winter, a portion of a swede turnip or a piece of carrot; that will do for the morning feed of one day. In the evening, feed about seven o'clock upon whole oats, if the animals be full grown or almost matured, as I have found them waste less of these than of any other description. Young rabbits, up to three months, may have crushed oats and a little bran, as their teeth are less able to masticate the hard whole grain. In the morning of another day give a handful of sweet meadow hay or dry clover, oats, and a little fine bran, turnip, beetroot, or carrot, and in the evening oats may again be given. It should be remembered that variety is of great importance. Peas soaked for twelve or fifteen hours may be given on the morning of the third day, but the water in which they have remained must be poured off, as the quantity absorbed will be quite sufficient as moisture; about two table-spoonsful of these peas may be allowed to each adult rabbit per diem, but to the larger varieties you may give a little more. Too many peas so prepared are not beneficial to the health, as they tend to swell more than fatten; yet they possess the latter property if given with care. Evening feed, oats, and a little turnip or carrot. Morning again, turnips and mangold, with a little bran and oats, not forgetting some hay, which, if they do not care to eat, is almost as inexpensive as oat straw, and will serve for bedding. Evening, especially if cold weather, give them a supper of "porridge," made of Indian meal—boiled, I prefer, but scalded is less trouble—which, if not too thin or too hot is good and wholesome, If a change to barley meal be made at times it will be beneficial, or pollard is by no means objectionable to them. A feed of potatoes or clean parings, well boiled, with the water drained from them makes an excellent feed once a week for variety, not forgetting to mix well with Indian or barley meal. The latter may be used more frequently if the whole grain is not very freely given, for, in consequence of its heating nature, it requires to be dealt out with a more niggardly hand than oats. With the potatoes prepared as before described, a handful of crushed linseed or oil cake may be given, say in a feed for thirty rabbits, as either of these tend to fatten; yet, being a slight aperient, too liberal a supply would derange the bowels. Brewers' grains may at times be given. It is true an amount of saccharine is there, yet the excess of moisture tends to counteract the fattening property, and so eventually tends to waste rather than otherwise. If given at all, they should be well squeezed in order to render them as dry as possible, and well mixed with Indian meal, and only given in very small quantities once a month. I by no means advocate them; I speak from experience, as I have tried them upon rabbits of all ages.

Mr. T. C. Lord, of Huddersfield, says: "I find, as a rule, that rabbits will eat greedily of their food for a few minutes after it is put in the trough, and then leave it, and in some cases will not touch it again till there is some fresh put in, which I think goes a long way to prove that the best plan is to feed them oftener, and give less food at a time. I feed my rabbits at least three times a day, giving for the first meal (which should be about half past seven in the morning) a handful of sweet hay and a small quantity of scalded meal. The scalded meal should not have too much water in it, that is to say, it should not be mixed too thin, as rabbits do not like it in this way; it should be mixed so that it will crumble, and the best way is to give it directly it is made, as it warms the rabbit, and has a better tendency to fatten. For the second meal, about one o'clock at noon, I give green food or carrots, which have a tendency to keep the bowels open, and for the third, six o'clock in the evening, oats or other grain. The meal for the first feed can be changed every alternate week, or oftener than that if thought advisable, and substituted by any of the following: barley meal and Indian corn, mixed; barley meal and coarse or fine sharps (pollard) mixed, or oatmeal and bran; but these must be scalded as before stated. A small portion of sulphur may be added, say once a week, as it keeps the bowels open and prevents pot belly and scurvy, or dry rot. A little linseed meal is also good when given occasionally with the porridge. For green food, vegetables, roots, &c., I give cabbage, lettuce, endive, parsley, chicory tops, carrot and turnip tops, carrots, kohl rabi, and potatoes. The latter should be boiled, and not given too often, as they have a tendency to fill the animal with wind. Soaked grey peas are also very good when not given too often. For grain, I give crushed oats, barley, or wheat, and these, if boiled occasionally, will be found to have a very beneficial effect. Brewers grains I decidedly object to, as they are apt to turn sour on the stomach, and thus do the animal a serious injury. As an instance of what my way of feeding will do, I may here state that I had a rabbit which, although very large, only weighed 10½lb. before I commenced feeding her on this system, but eight or ten days after she had increased fully 2lb. in weight."

Naturally, the rabbit will, as we all know, eat almost anything herbaceous, and has a taste for almost all vegetables in which it can freely indulge in its wild state. Yet such may not be given to them when domesticated, for, lacking the exercise afforded in the wild state, we must treat them accordingly. In the summer time, when green clover, vetches, &c., are plentiful, and consequently inexpensive, then is the time generally that our pets are "overdone" with green food, and suffer in proportion. That can never be cheap food, even if presented to you free of cost, by the eating of which your rabbits are injured, and require a week or two of very careful treatment and recourse to the "medicine chest" for restoration to health, to say nothing about the extra trouble and anxiety given. A little clover and vetches may be given once a day, but in small quantities; not with the same lavish hand that throws them the hay. Chicory tops are good, and I have used them as green food almost exclusively in summer as an experiment, and found them answer well. This food is not always to be had, except you are fortunate enough to have a large garden. Large beds of it can then be sown, and when the plants are 6in. or 8in. high they may be cut, and they will soon grow again, and bear cutting three or four times during the summer, especially if a wet one; and after two years the roots may be taken up in November, washed, and given with swedes and carrots. The common dock is not as good for rabbits as other green food, such as dandelion, &c., yet it is not decidedly injurious, though I do not recommend it as a general herbaceous food, whilst there are so many other leaves, &c., that are more beneficial as a daily diet during the summer. Avoid giving any green food when wet, as that will give the strongest rabbit the "rot," so called, or wasting of the bowels. All green food is best cut before sunset, or the fall of dew upon it, and spread out, not packed close, as it will heat, unless it is very dry, and so destroy the fresh flavour so desirable for the rabbits. The dandelion is valuable for rabbits, and those residing in the country are in this respect fortunate. As a rule too much green food is incautiously given by country fanciers because of its abundance; and there is no doubt that "dry food" feeding is the best and safest, and upon it the rabbits thrive better, more are reared, and are consequently eventually the cheapest.

Food too moist, as a rule, is not good, yet I by no means advocate the entire absence of fluids, especially towards the end of the winter, when the various roots used as food during the last three or four months have lost that juicy moisture so abundant in October and November when first stored. Milk and water just warm (the more of the former the better) is by no means objectionable to the palate of the most dainty rabbit; yet, perhaps the greater number would prefer a "sip" of cold water, of which perhaps two tablespoonfuls once a week may be given. A correspondent tells me that during the whole of one winter he gave his breeding does as much lukewarm milk as they would drink whilst he was looking on, both morning and night, and found that they did excellently on it, always looking for the milk before they touched any other portion of their food; and that he found that in winter it was a very good plan to mix a little barley flour with warm milk, and give it to them.

It is during the latter part of the winter, or early spring, that soaked peas, already alluded to, may be more freely given, because of the moisture they contain. I consider that all kinds of mixtures of Indian meal, barley meal, or pollard, should be prepared a few hours before use, as they undoubtedly swell; and I prefer this process going on within the mixing trough rather than the stomach of the rabbit. The same remark may be applied to hot potato parings when given freely, and when in their hot steamy state, they are mixed with bran or meal, and given hot. In this Mr. T. C. Lord disagrees with me. He says: "I have tried both systems, and found that to give the food immediately after mixing, and whilst in a warm state, is the most beneficial and satisfactory. My reasons for saying this are as follows: After the food has become cold, I find, as a general rule, the animal does not eat it with half the relish that it does when given warm; also, that the swelling process mentioned goes on chiefly during the mixing, and what little, if any, which takes place after does not do the slightest injury. And, again, I consider that rabbits, when in a confined state, should have at least one warm meal during the day."

The use of very little bran as a food is rather to be commended than a too free use of it, as it contains probably less nutritious properties than would appear at first thought; if given at all, I advocate the finer kind, in small quantities, to be given dry. Yet there are times when this food may be given with advantage. A feed of boiled rice will be worth giving occasionally, say two or three times during a month, and will be an agreeable change, but it should be given in a rather dryer state than when used for domestic purposes. All rabbits will not eat it with the same avidity as other kinds of food; yet, given as an occasional meal, it will be found of importance, and worth considering as one of the many kinds of food used in the rabbitry, and, if purchased by the hundredweight, not extravagantly dear. A pan, with 6lb. at a boiling, may be divided amongst sixty or eighty rabbits for a feed, when I prefer its being given when almost cold, as it then becomes more solid.

I often think what an advantage it would be, if a more settled opinion could be established as to the general mode of feeding, and the temperature of rabbitries, as no doubt the want of this oneness of opinion on these two very important particulars is far too evident in the ailments and too often death of very valuable specimens when sent to other homes; and I think it only right and just for all who send any of their stock to another's rabbitry to furnish in detail the mode of treatment as to food given, temperature in which they have been accustomed to live (and here I may remark that no rabbitry should be without its thermometer), and if kept in (so called) "out-side hutches," or within the more comfortable area of some suitable building with thick brick walls.

Amongst condiments, of which their name may be said to be legion, now claiming the attention of all stock-keepers, some, perhaps many, possess ingredients of a beneficial nature to rabbits, particularly to those not in very good health, resulting from improper treatment as to condition or quantity of food given. In such cases, anything of an attractive nature may be resorted to in the form of condiments, but it should only be mixed at the time of giving the feed; or, at most, you may mix the condiment in the whole at first when preparing, say as much food (such as potato parings in meal, as spoken of) as will serve for two feeds. I have found rabbits refuse the second feed so previously prepared, and can attribute it only to the fact that the condiment exposed to the air for some few hours becomes less palatable than when used fresh at each feed. All condiments are not the same in flavour after exposure to the air. I do not advocate a free and general use of such things, but when there is evidence that health is declining, a temporary resort to them is judicious.

The quantity of food requisite for each rabbit will soon be ascertained by observing the quantity left (if any) in the feeding trough; as a rule too much food is given, which is liable to waste. As to the question of feeding, a hint here may be of use. I never mix bran and oats together in the same feeding dish, for, as a rule, the latter is more sought for, and to find it the former is scratched out, more especially if the trough or dish is not of the right kind.

Rabbits should always have enough food to last from one meal to another, more especially is this necessary with does that are suckling, and young ones growing. Two feeds each day, as a rule, will be sufficient, say eight a.m. and six p.m., yet in some cases three times would be better, and it will soon be seen what they require without wasting. Few would imagine the difference in appearance between two rabbits as the result of diffcrent feeding; the one thin and lank, half wasted away with an excess of green food, which it will eat with a greediness, even if almost dying in consequence; yet the other specimen gives evidence by its whole appearance in general, and smooth glossy fur in particular, of the advantages of the dry food system.

I have often heard the remark "my rabbits waste more than they eat, and cost more than they ought by a great deal." This will not be the case if proper dishes are used. I give illustrations of the kinds which experience in their use has convinced me are the best for all purposes. Fig. 6 was made for me, and being circular, it may perhaps claim some little originality, and, without egotism, I think it the most economical kind ever seen in use, as it keeps the food clean, and prevents the rabbits sitting in it, which they will do if not prevented by some means. It may be made any size according to the number of rabbits in the hutch, and, as will be seen, it is intended for a number surrounding it. A dish 10in. in diameter, has the upper edge turned over ¾in. to prevent the food being scratched out, and is 1½in. deep at the lowest part of the hollow (I prefer the hollow, or concave form, for all feeding troughs or dishes, because of the greater difficulty the rabbit finds in scratching out the food), and from the turned-over edge to the cylinder or receptacle for the corn, &c., there is a space of 2in. The cylinder is 4½in. in diameter, and 3½in. high, exclusive of lid, and has inside a cone-shaped piece of tin, the base of which is rather less in diameter than that of the cylinder, which acts as a

Fig. 6.

director of the grain into the outer part of the dish. The cylinder is raised ⅜in. from the dish by three supports, to allow the food to find its way into the dish, as that previously there is consumed by the rabbits. The principle is, in fact, very much that of the bird or poultry fountain ordinarily in use. A lid to the top of the cylinder is of little importance; I have in use those with and without. At the bottom a piece of lead or other weighty substance should be fastened to prevent it being upset, which is impossible with this precaution. Such a trough will contain abundant food for, say six or eight half-grown rabbits for a day's feed. For young rabbits, from two to six months old, I do not have the dishes made so wide as 2in. from the cylinder, 1½in. will do; for, if too great a space is given, they will try to sit in the dish. Where more than six or eight rabbits are kept together (which is seldom the case if large), a larger-sized trough must of course be used, yet the 2in. space should be found sufficient for any size of dish and cylinder. A similar trough may be used of hexagon shape—yet I prefer the round one, though costing 1s. or 1s. 3d. more for extra labour, as all sharp edges and corners are avoided, which is always desirable, as rabbits are not then liable to injure themselves with them when capering about. As this kind of trough is for dry food only, all

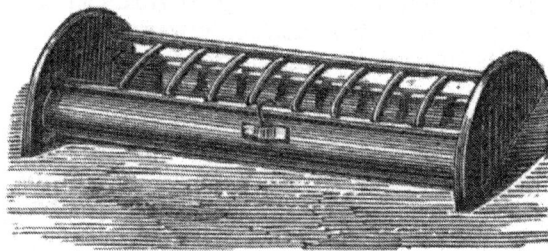

Fig. 7.

other kinds, in the form of paste, &c., should be put into a separate dish outside. Fig. 7 is a useful trough, and may be made any length according to the number of rabbits to use it. The size I use is 18in. long, 4in. across from inside of rounded edge (as a preventative to the food being scratched out, as alluded to in the other dish),

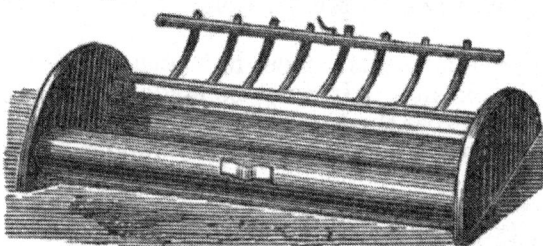

Fig. 8.

2in. deep, concave in shape, and the bars semicircular, as the rabbits then find a difficulty in sitting upon them. These bars are a little more than one-eighth of an inch thick, 2in. apart, attached to two strong ¼in. pieces hinged as frame, and a little hook to keep it down, as seen in the illustration. Fig. 8 is the

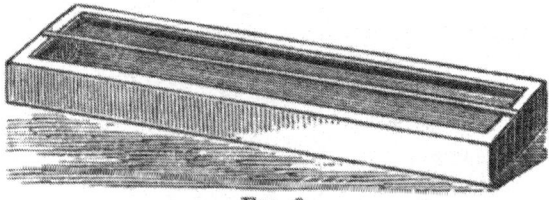

Fig. 9.

same trough opened. All these are made of zinc, which I prefer, as being clean and easily washed; and feeding dishes of all kinds should be kept sweet and clean, especially in hot weather, or any moist food used is liable to turn sour; this is of great importance, and the neglect of this little attention will prevent many a rabbit from enjoying or even eating its food. Fig. 9 may be made of

D

wood, concave as the others, 3½in. or 4in. across, and with a wire, ¼in. thick, running in the centre from end to end, so as to prevent the food being soiled. This is a cheap trough, yet it may be found of use; and if made of wood, the upper edges should be protected by slips of zinc, tacked on, as alluded to in reference to other woodwork edges exposed to the teeth of the rabbits. The common cast-iron spittoon is of the right shape as regards the incline of the sides towards the centre. This incline, however, should not be too great, or the rabbits, especially the large ones with broad noses, cannot feed, and the food will consequently be found tucked away under the sides of the dish, and beyond the reach of the animals' teeth. These dishes are useful for one or two rabbits in a hutch, are cheap, from 4d. to 5d. each, and cannot be upset, or the food easily scratched out. I have tried racks for hay, but by no means recommend them, except in some cases, because the rabbits are liable to injure themselves by running against them when frisking about, and I have had more than one valuable animal suffer in consequence. As hay is generally cheap enough, and, if of the right quality, sweet and aromatic, the rabbits will not refuse to eat it from the floor, which should never be in such a state from one day to another as to soil it. The feeding troughs, such as I have illustrated, are made by Mr. D. Reid, Hilton-street, Oldham-street, Manchester.

Mr. T. C. Lord recommends a trough, "both simple in construction and economical in use. It must be made of tin, about 12in. in length, 3in. wide across the top, and 2in. deep in the centre, and the same shape as shown in Fig. 10. It should have pieces of

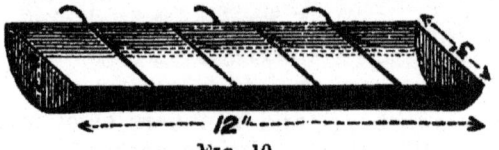

Fig. 10.

wire soldered across the top at a distance of 3in. apart, which prevent the rabbits from scratching out or otherwise spoiling their food. This kind of trough will be found very serviceable." For

Fig. 11.

holding hay he advises the use of a rack, such as shown in Fig. 11, but, as I have already said, I do not approve of them.

CHAPTER IV.

DISINFECTANTS, VENTILATION, AND TEMPERATURE.

To insure the health of the rabbits, I recommend that hutches placed in so close a position as to destroy all chance of a free current of air passing through should be so arranged that they can periodically be brought into the open air for a few days, and, if necessary, purified with an application of whitewash. If the hutch is one of a stack in an inside or "fit-up" rabbitry, and is what may be called a "fixture," then other means should be resorted to, in order to make it properly pure. I have tried several things as purifiers and disinfectants, and decidedly prefer those in the form of powder, yet the liquids and carbolics are by no means objectionable, except that they add to the dampness of the floor caused by the urine; but when the floors are washed with a solution of lime and water, and allowed to dry, they are then ready for use. To burn brown or any coarse paper in the hutch once a month tends to purify and to remove the impure gases, and after this fumigation an evident freshness is perceptible; in the warm weather this is especially requisite. I see no reason why any rabbitry with its sixty to eighty rabbits within its walls should not, with due care, be as inoffensive to the olfactory nerves as any well arranged stable in the care of a competent groom; and I may here state that when rabbits are well cared for, and in the hands of those studying their health, they are by no means the offensive pets some would have us suppose. After a hutch has been cleaned, a sprinkling of pine sawdust, which contains much turpentine, is useful, and acts as a disinfectant to a certain extent.

Ventilation is of vast importance, more especially to those "inside hutches" where the air is probably only admitted through a door or window. A ventilator through the roof is an advantage if placed sufficiently high above the top tier of hutches for the rabbits to escape the strong draught; and if the external air blowing down upon them be too strong, it should be regulated accordingly. There is no doubt that the want of a sufficient supply of pure air is the cause of many diseases to which rabbits are liable in confined hutches; cold air is not desirable, yet pure air is essential. My own experience proves that certain kinds of rabbits, such as Belgian hares, Patagonians, and silver greys, are more succesfully reared in open outside hutches. I have found animals so kept less liable to those complaints which are more generally found in closer confined hutches, and, as a rule, such animals so reared present a more lively appearance. Of course they must be protected from damp as much as possible, and the wire portion of the hutch should be furnished with shutters or curtains for use during cold winds, which are objectionable, especially if blowing direct in front of the hutch; all ventilation should be above the rabbits.

Temperature is also of some importance to the health and hardy constitution of rabbits. Yet all varieties cannot be treated in the same manner, the "lops," of all others, should have the highest rate. I have found that about 60° is probably a fair average, and that such temperature is most suitable for the successful rearing of lops, and tends best to produce the size of ear so desirable in this variety, and I have ascertained from some of the most successful breeders of lops that about this rate of temperature is what they also prefer; yet for other varieties a lower rate is more desirable. My rabbitry, containing Angoras, Dutch, Himalayan, Polish, and Siberian, is kept as near as possible at about 50°, and the lops, as stated, in the higher temperature; whilst the Belgians, Patagonians, and silver greys are in outside hutches in all seasons, and do well, and I find if they are slightly suffering, as they will at times, from the inclemency of weather, they soon recover, as they are more hardy, and are by no means so easily affected by change of temperature as the other varieties. Every rabbitry should have its thermometer for reference, and it will be found invaluable; and though in all probability one uniform rate of temperature cannot always be maintained, yet as near an approach to the standard as possible will be found an advantage. Rabbits are not liable to numerous diseases if they are kept with due care; yet, if the requisite attentions are denied, and the rules laid down for their treatment disregarded, a variety of ailments will be the result.

ADVERTISEMENTS.

BOOKS PUBLISHED BY HORACE COX,
AT 346, STRAND, W.C.

THE IDSTONE PAPERS.—A Series of Articles and Desultory Observations on Sport and Things in General, written originally for *The Field* newspaper. Large post 8vo., price 7s. 6d.

THE DIAMOND DIGGINGS of SOUTH AFRICA.—A Personal and Practical Account. By "SARCELLE," of *The Field*. With a Brief Notice of the New Gold Fields. With Map, large post 8vo., price 6s.

ROUND the TABLE; or, Notes on Cookery and Plain Recipes, with a Selection of Bills of Fare. By "The G. C." All its recipes have been tested by experience, and are so given as to be intelligible of themselves, the object being not so much to provide a volume of reference for a professed cook as to explain how, with ordinary resources, an artistic dinner can be produced. Post 8vo., price 6s.

SECOND EDITION of the DOGS of the BRITISH ISLANDS. Edited by "STONEHENGE." Greatly enlarged (including new Parts on "Kennel Management of Dogs," and "Judging at Dog Shows and Field Trials"). 4to., gilt edges, toned paper, price 10s. 6d.

THE SILKWORM BOOK; or, Silkworms Ancient and Modern, their Food and Mode of Management. In demy 8vo., price 2s. 6d., cloth gilt; post free, 2s. 8d.

THE RURAL ALMANAC and SPORTSMAN'S ILLUSTRATED CALENDAR for 1873. Price 1s.; by post, 1s. 2d. [*Nearly ready.*

THE ANGLER'S DIARY, wherein the Angler can Register his Take of Fish throughout the Year. An extensive List of Fishing Stations throughout the World is added. In cloth, crown 4to., price 1s. 6d., post free 1s. 8d.

THE SHOOTER'S DIARY for 1872-73 contains Forms for Registering Game killed during the Year, either by a Single Gun or by a Party, or off the whole Estate. A List of Shooting Stations throughout the World is also given. Crown 4to., price 1s. 6d.; post free 2d. extra.

FACTS and USEFUL HINTS relating to FISHING and SHOOTING, Illustrated; being a Collection of Information and Recipes of the greatest utility to the general Sportsman, to which is added a Series of Recipes on the Management of Dogs in Health and Disease. Second Edition, enlarged and revised. Large post 8vo., price 5s. cloth.

THE COUNTRY HOUSE; a Collection of Useful Information and Recipes of the greatest utility to the housekeeper generally. Illustrated. Second Edition, enlarged and revised. Large post 8vo., price 5s. cloth.

THE FARM: being Part I. of the Second Edition of the FARM, GARDEN, STABLE, and AVIARY. Valuable to country gentlemen, farmers, &c. Large post 8vo., price 5s.

THE GARDEN: being Part II. of the Second Edition of the FARM, GARDEN, STABLE, and AVIARY. Large post 8vo., price 5s.

THE STABLE: being Part III. of the Second Edition of the FARM, GARDEN, STABLE, and AVIARY. Large post 8vo., price 5s.

The Bazaar, The Exchange and Mart, and Journal of the Household.

ILLUSTRATED.

EVERY WEEK: PRICE TWOPENCE.

GENERAL CONTENTS.

THE DRAWING ROOM.—Résumés of Dramatic, Art, Scientific, and Musical news of the week; Critiques on New Music; Articles on Art Subjects, &c., &c.

THE HALL.—Articles upon Canaries and all other Cage Birds; British Seaweeds; Management of Pets; Notes on Places at Home and Abroad; Miscellaneous Articles upon Subjects of General Interest.

THE LIBRARY.—Articles upon the Noteworthy Books recently published; Notes upon Various Literary Subjects.

THE WORKSHOP.—Articles and Notes upon Various Branches of Amateur Mechanics.

THE HOUSEKEEPER'S ROOM.—Articles upon Domestic Matters, Recipes of all kinds, &c.

THE BOUDOIR.—Notes on Present Fashions; Honiton Lace making; Fancy Work of different kinds.

THE GARDEN.—Articles upon the Cultivation of Flowers, Fruit, and Vegetables; British Ferns; Garden Operations; Bee Keeping, &c.

THE CURTILAGE.—Articles on Diseases of Dogs; Exhibition Rabbits; Farming; Poultry; Pigeons; Reports of Poultry, Pigeon, and Rabbit Shows.

COMING EVENTS.—Notice of the dates of all coming Public Concerts, Exhibitions, Sporting Contests, &c.

EXCHANGE AND MART.—Thousands of Articles of *every* description for Exchange, or Sale, or Wanted by *private persons*.

WANTS AND VACANCIES.—Governesses, Tutors, Clerks, Servants, and others Wanting Situations, and Situations Vacant.

Quarterly Subscription, 2s. 8d., post paid.

May be had at the Railway Bookstalls, and from all Respectable Newsagents.

LONDON OFFICE: 32, WELLINGTON-STREET, STRAND, W.C.

Rabbits For Prizes and Profit.

PART II.

GENERAL MANAGEMENT.
PART II.

By CHARLES RAYSON.

ILLUSTRATED.

LONDON:
"THE BAZAAR" OFFICE, 32, WELLINGTON-STREET, STRAND, W.C.

PRICE SIXPENCE.

ADVERTISEMENTS.

NET MAKERS TO HER MAJESTY THE QUEEN.

NEW GARDEN NETS, TENTS, MARQUEES, and RICK CLOTHS.

A good Second-hand Garden Net, 4yds. wide, 28s., 2yds. 14s., the 100yds. run; large size Purse Nets, 7s. per dozen; large size Gamekeepers' Capes, lined, 12s. 6d., unlined, 7s. 6d.

Rabbit Nets, corded ready for use, for shooting or catching.

Hay Cloths, Tarpaulins, and Cart Covers; also, Bird, Pheasant, Poultry, and Fishing Nets of every description.

J. ALLEN and SON, Manufacturers,
11, SEYMOUR-STREET, EUSTON-ROAD, LONDON, N.W.

RABBITS.

MESSRS. THOS. C. and H. LORD have, during the greater part of the Season, a number of Rabbits surplus over those they keep for Exhibition, which they are willing to sell at moderate prices. The stock includes Lops, Silver Greys, Himalayans, Angoras, and Dutch, many of them prize winners, and fit for exhibition—same strain as their noted "Champions," which have won so many Silver Cups, Medals, and other Prizes at the principal Shows throughout the Kingdom.

MR. A. H. EASTEN, of Rutland Villa, Botanic-lane, Hull, has continually Surplus Stock from his celebrated LOP-EARED, HIMALAYA, and other RABBITS, of prize strains, which he will sell at reasonable rates, according to age.—Prices and full particulars on application.

LOP-EARED RABBITS.

MR. E. FROST, of Hackbridge, Carshalton, Surrey, has generally a quantity of these RABBITS for disposal. They are from the best prize-winning strains in the country. The price varies according to age, length of ear, &c.—Full particulars will be forwarded on receipt of letter.

FANCY PRIZE RABBITS, of every variety kept in this country, from my well-known Stock (which I keep for amusement), of which at times I have more than I care to have, and shall be glad to spare a few specimens to those desirous of improving their Stock.—CHARLES RAYSON, Esq., Ivy Lodge, Sidsbury, near Manchester.

WM. WHITWORTH, Jun., 30, Birch-lane, Longsight, Manchester, will have some Young Ones to SELL from all his PRIZE RABBITS (Angora, Himalayan, Patagonian or Andalusian, Belgian Hare, and Dutch), at prices according to quality and age.

SECOND EDITION. Large post 8vo., price 6d.

BREEDING POULTRY FOR PRIZES—Being full directions for the proper selection of stock birds, the points required, &c., for the successful production of prize poultry, and numerous first-class wood engravings of fowls and feathers, showing the shapes and markings that must be aimed at. By JAMES LONG (winner of the New York Poultry Society's Prize for the best "Thesis on the Breeding and Management of Poultry").

Large post 8vo., price 6d.

EXHIBITION POULTRY (Part I.)—Being minute and accurate descriptions of Cochins, Dorkings, Spanish, Brahmas, French Fowl, Game, and their varieties, such as they must be to entitle them to success in the show pen. By JAMES LONG. Illustrated with four full-page portraits of prize birds.

Large post 8vo., price 6d.

EXHIBITION POULTRY (Part II.)—Being minute and accurate descriptions of Hamburghs, Polands, Malays, Bantams, "Any other Varieties," and Turkeys, such as they must be to entitle them to success in the show pen. By JAMES LONG. Illustrated with four full-page portraits of prize winners.

"THE BAZAAR" OFFICE, 32, WELLINGTON STREET, LONDON, W.C.

THE DUTCH RABBIT.

CHAPTER V.

DISEASES AND THEIR TREATMENT.

Rabbits by nature are endowed with strong and hardy constitutions, yet when in domestication they are attacked by any complaints, these are generally of a serious kind, and, without prompt attention, soon terminate fatally. Some animals are much more liable to disease than others, and so become a constant care; others I have half a dozen years old, which never have been unwilling to eat; and that, as a general rule, is the best test of a rabbit's health. It is only when they are too quiet, sitting in the corner of the hutch, and seeming to manifest no anxiety about the feeding time, that sickness should be expected. It is rare that a rabbit in health, even with its feeding trough by no means empty, will not caper about, and seem to remind its owner that it will be in want of food. Some diseases or complaints are much more easily cured than others, and frequently the most troublesome to treat are the less serious in their nature, whilst at times a complaint from which a rabbit is suffering for the first time proves fatal. One thing is certain, that the old adage, "Prevention is better than cure," is applicable to the well-being of rabbits. All complaints treated in time or when in the first stages, are more likely to give favourable results, and save a great amount of anxiety and trouble, than if they were allowed to go for some time unheeded. Every rabbitry should contain its "medicine chest," but the less demand there is upon its resources the better. All rabbits suffering from mange, scurf, snuffles, or other contagious or infectious complaint, should at once be separated from the others, and all feeding troughs washed, and the interior of hutches whitewashed before being again used. Sickly rabbits are always best alone, as they can receive that special care so essential to their recovery, and they will not be disturbed by the movements of the others.

Canker in Ear.—Symptoms: A thick yellow discharge from the inside of the ears, which appears to proceed from some disease in the head; the eye on that side appears to be very weak, with a slight discharge; the rabbit loses condition, and does not relish its food.

The discharge from the ear arises from ulceration in the deep recess, and is difficult to cure. Remedy: Clear out the discharge by a little pressure, and a sponge or soft rag soaked in warm water, avoiding any of the latter falling into the ear, and when dry applying a lotion, obtained at any veterinary surgeon, to whom the rabbit should be shown, and who will, if surgical aid is requisite for any operation, perform it more successfully than would less experienced hands. Feed upon the best food; and extra care in this respect will be required, for if the rabbit becomes weak its chances of recovery are very slight. In similar cases in dogs the following has proved curative, and favourable results might be expected from it with rabbits: Mercurius (mercury) trituration No. 3, dose one grain, or as much as will cover a threepenny piece, not piled up, twice a day. Decrease doses as improvement takes place. Obtain 6d. bottle by post from Turner & Co., Fleet Street, London. Well wash out discharge with lukewarm water.

Constipation.—This is a complaint seldom observed, and is not generally very difficult to cure. It is caused by an excess of dry food, without a proper allowance of water or other liquid. The rabbit so suffering may be seen sitting quiet in some corner of the hutch, and seeming regardless of food, and sometimes the body is swollen. If it should be with others remove it, as being more convenient for applying restoratives which should not be partaken of by the others. Remedy: Keep the rabbit warm and dry; supply it with green food, as clover vetches, chicory tops, and even a cabbage leaf or two (objectionable, however, as they are to rabbits in health) will be found beneficial, and as greens of this kind are always acceptable to rabbits, there is little fear of their not eating them; yet caution must be exercised in not allowing too many, and when they have accomplished their purpose must be gradually discontinued, and the more general mode of treatment and feeding resorted to again. Should this vegetable diet fail in a day or two to produce the desired result, a more powerful remedy may be tried, as a little salt and water, which at this time will be drunk with an apparent relish, or you may dissolve twelve drachms of Glauber salts in a pint of water, and give two tablespoonfuls twice a day. Generally three or four doses will accomplish all that is requisite.

Diseased Liver.—Rabbits suffering from this complaint are by no means easy to cure, and I strongly urge the importance of judicious feeding as the most certain preventive. This attack upon the liver is caused by a small parasite, generally named "fluke," which attaches itself to the liver and causes it to decay, and eventually become almost rotten. It seems probable that the eggs or germs of these pests are received into the stomach with some vegetables to which they are attached, and only cause mischief when the digestive organs are not in a strong and healthy state. It may easily be known that a rabbit suffers from this complaint by the difficulty the animal has in breathing, which is heavy, and at times accompanied by an audible noise, yet the patient eats and seems otherwise to present almost the same appearance as if in health, and does will rear their litters when thus attacked; but, as may be supposed, the offspring are not so strong and healthy as those born under more favourable circumstances. If the rabbit be of little value, I should advise its being killed at once; but if a valuable one, to try to cure, or at least retard the progress of the disease, may be worth the trial. Remedy: First ascertain that the appetite and digestive organs are in a healthy state, and give one grain of calomel in two doses, at intervals of twelve hours, and with fresh air and clean hutch an improvement will be the result.

Dropsy, or " Pot Belly."—This disease is peculiar to young rabbits from six weeks to six months old, and is caused by a hutch too limited in size (and that often dark and damp), combined with an excess of damp green food, without a proportionate allowance of the more solid and dry; and so the body of the animal becomes swollen in the lower part. It will eat with an appetite indicating perfect health for awhile, yet if left unnoticed, or no means resorted to for its recovery, its relish for food lessens and it will pine away. Remedy: Separate it from the others, and give plenty of room for exercise; a run upon the dry ground for an hour or two each day in warm weather will be found beneficial. Give dry food, as barley, oats, split peas, malt coomes, leaves of the oak tree dried; and after a few days of this regimen, a little water may be given; also a sprig or two of sage, parsley, or thyme. Carrots will be found advantageous if in small quanties, but they must be given sparingly, as it is known that the too free indulgence in succulent diet is the cause of the mischief. This complaint is seldom noticed in the rabbitry of an experienced fancier, as experience says that dry food is the most safe and economical. All experience goes to prove that food must be the cheapest which in its use maintains the consumer in perfect health.

Ear Gum, or Wax.—This complaint is not (except in cases of total neglect) fatal to rabbits, but seems very troublesome to some animals. Some seem never to have their cars made sore by it, but to have them always filled up with scabby excrescences clinging to the interior, for which very little positive cause can be assigned, for with rabbits of the same litter and in the same hutch, and consequently with the same treatment, it will be found that some are always perfectly free, and with ears always clean, whilst the others require constant attention and treatment for its removal. As a general rule, the ears of rabbits should be occasionally examined, in order to keep them as free as possible from such attacks. At times I have thought that short and erect-eared rabbits were more liable to it than those with lop or hanging ears, and wondered if any falling dust from any imperfect floor of hutch overhead, which erect ears might receive, acted as a germ or nucleus of such unwelcome collection; but experiments have not convinced me of the truth of this supposition. When the ears are so encumbered, the rabbit, it will be observed, seems to avoid being handled by them, and shrinks as with pain, which is evidently experienced. Remedy: The most simple and effective remedy is to remove or loosen the wax with the quill end of a feather, or other blunt smooth instrument, avoiding the giving of pain as much as possible. Allow the rabbit to shake out the loose particles, and then sprinkle into the ear, as far down the socket as convenient, flour of sulphur; repeat this two or three times at intervals of three days, and probably without further aid from the quill, except it be to remove some large piece deep in the ear, the cure will be complete, and many months may occur before such attention is again requisite.

Eruptions.—These appear like a white scurf, but upon examination will be found to be little sores, which cause the hair to come off. Remedy: Apply to the part affected, a thin ointment of lard, flour of sulphur, and a little carbolic acid, all well mixed, and used every other day. If at all like boils, requiring relief when ripe, the lancet in skilful hands would be the most effectual, but I do not advocate its use except in a real case of need. The impurity of the air in which the rabbit lives frequently causes such appearances. The hair will grow again when the blood is more pure and skin free from the eruptions. Keep the patient warm, yet allow plenty of fresh air, and a cure will be effected in a short time.

Fits, Megrims, or Dizziness.—It is not very often that rabbits are so affected, yet when such is the case it is only too evident by the manner in which the head is held (which is generally leaning on one side as if a stiff neck were the cause), a wildness about the eye is observable, the limbs are weak, and the animal seems to stagger in moving; when taken up it will apparently swing about in the hand, and when placed upon the ground roll over several times in the most frantic manner, as if suffering the most acute pain, and after several convulsive struggles lie as if perfectly exhausted, with one cheek upon the ground, and the whole head distorted so as to present anything but an agreeable appearance. The cause may generally be attributed to a defect in the digestive organs, from which the stomach becomes over weighted with food (for generally the rabbit will keep eating, suffering as it is), and, digestion being imperfect, such results follow. When the attack is treated in its early stages it is seldom fatal, except in old rabbits, yet I have known does suffering three weeks with such attacks, and after recovery give birth to several litters, and perhaps the only indication observable was that the head was not held quite straight afterwards. Remedy: The rabbit should be kept warm, yet not too close, for free access of fresh air is essential to its recovery; administer 4gr. of powdered camphor in two teaspoonfuls of tepid water every day for a week, if requisite to do so for that length of time; but probably after the fourth day an evident change will be found for the better, and the head will be held more in the natural position, and a firmness in the limbs, as when in health, will be observed. When these favourable symptoms are presented, apply the camphor every third day for a week or so more, and in a smaller quantity until perfect health is restored. Give a liberal supply of herbaceous food (if to be had), as green clover, dandelion, turnip tops, and do not forget a little sweet hay and crushed oats. When the bowels are in a healthy state there will not be much to fear.

Inflammation of Uterus.—This occurs at times to does when the requisite discretion is not used in pairing them, and what was said in a previous page in reference to this subject—" breeding and rearing "—should be observed, and then little danger need be apprehended of the rabbits being troubled with this complaint. It is by no means incurable, yet it is the work of a few weeks, especially if not observed in time. Remedy: Keep such rabbits alone, give a liberal supply of food of the right kind, and apply the undermentioned lotion with a sponge to the part affected, once a day for three days, then every other day, and less frequent as the inflammation disappears, which after three or four applications should be the case; and as the natural appearance is presented, a little further attention at intervals will effect the desired restoration to health. Lotion: 1 drachm sulphate of zinc, 1 drachm laudanum, dissolved in pint of spring water. As this is poisonous, care should be taken in its use, and the rabbit should be held for a few minutes to prevent its licking any off. Another lotion will also be found of benefit to a rabbit so suffering: 2 drachms Goulard's extract, 1 drachm laudanum, to 1 pint of water, applied as the previous one. The first is what I more particularly recommend for its speedy effect, yet it requires more caution in its use; but both are valuable.

Insects.—Rabbits so troubled are most frequently those inhabiting cold damp hutches, which are seldom cleaned and purified, and those constantly lying upon damp and half fermented bedding, from which arise unhealthy warm vapours, and these causes, combined with a too watery green food diet, will produce these unwelcome visitors, which will generally be found around the ears and forehead. I have seen rabbits almost covered with them, and when thus irritated they present a dull, and often thin and inanimate appearance, as if not well fed. Remedy: Cut the hair shorter in those places most infested as this will facilitate the application of a sprinkling of sulphur (which to the skin is always beneficial), which should be rubbed well down to the roots of the hair; or fumigate the hair with strong tobacco smoke, protecting the eyes and nose as much as possible. Apply also a sprinkling of white hellebore, which, if blown through a small bellows (to be obtained at any chemist's at a cost of sixpence, as used for insect powders), will be forced to the roots of the hair, and a few applications will generally exterminate the insects. The Insecticide Vicat is a good remedy, and penny-royal in the bedding is a simple and sure prevention.

Looseness, or Disease of the Bowels.—This very frequent ailment is generally observed in the rabbitries of those near an abundance of green food, which, when given without the requisite care as to it fitness and limit, almost invariably produces this result. Rabbits when suffering from this complaint usually become sickly in appearance and thin, as if wasting away, which will be the case if prompt means are not resorted to. Remedy: Place the rabbit in a warm and comfortable hutch, supply it with dry food, as crushed oats and dry bran, amongst which mix a dozen crushed juniper berries; or mix a little oatmeal and peameal into a stiff paste, as a more general diet for a short time, until an evident change is observed in the dung. In the dry oats and bran may be mixed a powdered acorn of small size with each feed; as this is a valuable astringent, no medicine chest for the rabbitry should be without it. When a favourable change is seen, a little water may be given, as two tablespoonfuls every third day. Sweet hay will be found of advantage, and will be eaten freely. Care should be taken to apply the remedies on the first symptoms of the disease. Summer time is generally the season in which rabbits are most troubled, because (as before stated) of the abundance of green food at hand.

Loss of Appetite.—Various causes tend to a disregard for food, as cold, stomach or digestive organs disordered by receiving food injurious or in excess, when, instead of the usual eagerness for food at the usual time (which is a sure criterion that the rabbit is healthy), a total indifference is manifest, and a quietness is observed in its general manner. Remedy: In these cases a little stimulant may be resorted to—as a slice of toast soaked in ale, but if this is refused, you may warm the ale and give two tablespoonfuls twice a day, and probably two days of such attention will accomplish all that is requisite; or, instead of ale, elderberry wine will be found beneficial. When eating is resumed supply with a little milk and bread, carrots, oats, and other food most palatable, and but very little special care will be required for a few days longer.

Mange.—This differs in some respects from scurf in appearance. It is often caused by a too habitual feeding upon dry food, and is generally more troublesome in winter than in summer, when herbaceous plants and roots are not easily obtainable; or by hutches lacking proper ventilation and cleanliness. The appearance presented is that of a grey, scaly, hard skin at the roots of the hair, more perceptible to the eye than the touch, around the eyelids, nose, and at times the roots of the ears. Remedy: Sprinkle daily upon the parts affected flour of sulphur for a week, and, should this prove ineffectual, apply the ointments as applied to scurf; or, melt 4oz. of hogs' lard, with moderate heat, and add ½oz. of oil of vitriol; stir well together until cold, and apply for three or four days in succession. As this would prove injurious to the eyes, care must be used in its application. In places where the hair comes off by the application of such remedies, the following restorative will be found of use—1oz. of honey, ½oz. laurel oil, ½oz. linseed oil, and ½oz. of onion juice; mix well together, and apply every other day for a week. A decoction of birch is also a simple and effectual means for the purpose, and, if sulphur be given with the dry bran or oats at times, it will be of service; or rub a little sulphur upon the nose, roots of ears, and around the eyes, as it acts as a preventive to both scurf and mange, and as such is more important and far less troublesome than the most effectual cure.

Mr. T. C. Lord says: "I advise the following remedy, which I have found effectual in several exceedingly bad cases, and which has not the same tendency to turn the animal sickly as those mentioned by Mr. Rayson: Mix a small portion of black sulphur in lard till it forms a kind of salve or ointment, then rub the parts affected with it night and morning, taking care that it rubs off the scurf. The animal will in time lick the ointment off; therefore it does good as well internally as externally. Give the rabbit a good feed of sweet hay at least once a day, and a moderate supply of green food, as this disease often arises from the want of proper succulent food. Keep the hutch well cleaned out, and let it have a good supply of litter and a drink of acid milk once or twice a week." Mange being infectious, the affected animal should be isolated.

Matted Hair.—The best plan is to use the scissors just to open all the matted wool (avoiding injury to the skin), then with care and patience, with use of scissors and metal comb (which is the best for the purpose, being stronger than horn or tortoiseshell), the coat may be rendered clean again, but probably not before the skin is laid bare in places by the process, yet the wool will soon grow again if the rabbit is kept warm and well fed, which is requisite after the rather painful process. Angoras should be regularly attended to with the comb, in order to keep their wool from entanglement, and the more excellent the rabbit is in quality the larger the wool, and consequently more liable to become matted. This variety should not be crowded together in hutches, as that is the cause of the evil to a great extent.

Moulting.—Rabbits are, when about six weeks old, liable to this, which is not always passed through without serious, and, in numerous instances, fatal results. During this process of nature care should be taken to keep the rabbits warm, and I strongly recommend that they remain with the doe until they are almost safe through this trying ordeal, which will be generally about the eighth or tenth week, after which the chances are, that with due care and attention, the patients will pull through. Feed the doe well with good nutritious food, as that best tends to the strength of the young ones. It will be observed that the covering of fur at ten weeks is rather unlike that presented at three weeks, and this again is more down-like than that of the moulted rabbit. In the second covering there seems to be the fixed permanent shades of marking, from which little or no deviation is ever again perceptible, except in some few instances.

Ophthalmia.—This is more particularly observable in young rabbits, and is caused by the impurity of the hutch, and allowing the dung to remain until so saturated with urine that a strong ammoniacal gas or vapour is produced. The effect will be more generally observed in any hutch with insufficient ventilation, and in time the impurity becomes so great that disinfectants and the burning of paper as recommended will be found necessary, and for a while effectual. This must be resorted to whenever an offensive effluvia is perceptible, and to allow the hutch to remain unused for a few days will be found advantageous. The effect it produces upon the eyes of young rabbits, which are very tender, is to impart to them a sore swollen appearance, and an evident difficulty in opening; and at times they remain closed for several days. The eye also seems distended from its socket, and around the lid may be seen small red pimples, and these will also extend to the forehead, roots of ears, and neck. Remedy: Remove the patient; keep it in a warm, yet well-ventilated hutch, and apply with a sponge twice a day a little warm milk and water. For three or four days allow a liberal diet, and if no evidence of improvement is perceptible, as a last resource, apply to the parts affected with a sponge a solution, $\frac{1}{2}$oz. of white copperas to a pint of spring water; avoid giving pain as much as possible, for when the rabbit suffers from this complaint the eye is remarkably tender, and requires delicate treatment. Generally in a week or two a cure may be expected if applied in time.

Paralysis.—This disease generally attacks the hind quarters, and for a while renders the rabbit so powerless that its hind legs may be seen dragging along in the most pitiable state, and remain thus for days before a cure is effected. When such symptoms as want of activity in the extremities manifest themselves prompt measures should be resorted to, as every hour is of importance. The cause is frequently a damp hutch, more especially if it is stood upon the floor, and that unpaved or asphalted; and rabbits running upon damp floors will be found to be more liable than others to this serious disease, which at times is by no means easily cured. Rabbits even in well arranged hutches are also liable, though less so than the others. The disease may be attributed generally to a deficiency in the supply of nervous force in the parts affected. Remedy: 4grs. of camphor, 2grs. of sulphate of iron, mixed in a little powdered liquorice and treacle, and given in the form of a small pill every other day. Apply also along the spine, more particularly in the region of the loins, a little turpentine well rubbed in twice a week. To facilitate this process the hair may be cut short, especially if an Angora rabbit is the patient; the hair will soon grow again. I have tried a blister, which, if it can be retained in the right position, will be found of advantage, but I prefer the other remedies, as generally equally beneficial in result and more convenient in their application. The general health of the rabbit is tolerably good during the state of helplessness, and it will eat almost as usual, especially for the first few days, after which want of exercise tends to lessen its relish for food. It should be kept warm, and well supplied with the best and most nutritious food to aid the means used for its recovery. The attack lasts from six to ten days.

Pot-Belly.—(See under "Dropsy.")

Red Water, or Discoloured Urine.—This is a disease of the kidneys, which become inflamed, and though not often fatal, requires patience and care to effect a cure. It is caused generally by damp and exposure to cold; or, improper feeding tends also to produce this unusual appearance in the urine, which seems as if tinged with blood. Though the rabbit so troubled will generally continue to eat, yet it is not in appearance and manner quite so vivacious. Remedy: Place the rabbit in a warmer hutch, if the one it occupies is not the most comfortable; and supply with good farinaceous food—as oatmeal, boiled potatoes (given warm), a few oats, a little endive, dandelion, sow thistle, and carrots. Two tablespoonfuls of water in which bran has been soaked twenty-four hours may be given every day until the urine presents its natural appearance, generally from four to eight days.

Scurf.—This contagious complaint is a disease of the skin, which becomes rough to the touch, and is found more generally to attack rabbits confined in ill ventilated hutches, and most especially when too many are kept in one building, and not more frequently cleaned than others in "outside hutches." These latter, it will be found, are less liable to the attack of this troublesome disease. It presents itself on the nose, roots of ears, and eyelids, in fact its presence may be noticed almost all over the body. The rabbit has a rather more dull and heavy appearance of manner than usual, and if the attack be left uncared for, the rabbit will be sacrificed. The rabbit must be well fed, and with plenty of fresh air there is not much to fear, providing the disease is treated in its first stages. Directly the complaint makes its appearance, or is suspected, the patient should be placed in a hutch remote from the others. Remedies: First, tear in pieces an ounce of "Limerick roll" tobacco, pour upon it half a pint of hot water, and, when cool, add six grains of cayenne pepper, and, when well stirred together, apply with sponge to the roots of the hair where affected. Repeat this every other day, and on the second or third application the scurf will come off, and in all probability the hair will come with it; yet the latter will soon be restored. Another remedy is sulphur mixed with oil. Whale is the strongest, but rather too offensive in smell, and need seldom be resorted to, yet it is decided in effect. When of the consistency of a thin paste, apply it once every three days, rubbing it well down to the skin, removing the hair with scissors to facilitate the process. Sulphur mixed with lard is also effective as a cure, and more agreeable to the patient. Feed well upon moist food; keep the hutch well ventilated, for the want of this contributes greatly to this complaint. See also under "Mange."

Snuffles.—This complaint being infectious the rabbit affected should be removed from the neighbourhood of the healthy ones. In its symptoms the disease bears a strong resemblance to influenza in the human subject, and is to be attributed to the same cause, viz., exposure to cold. Rabbits in damp hutches without the requisite protection from cold draughts, are liable to this troublesome and often fatal complaint, which if not attended to as soon as observed, requires at times long and patient treatment. The rabbit is heard sneezing; a moisture at first is perceptible around the nostrils, which if left uncared for, eventually becomes of a thicker and glutinous consistency, and causes difficulty in breathing. Loss of appetite follows, and in a few days the nostrils are apparently closed with mucilage; inflammation of the lungs takes place frequently, and death is the result. Remedy: Let the rabbit be kept warm and secured from cold; give a few boiled potatoes with a little salt; barley meal mixed into a paste and given warm will be conducive to its recovery, and there must be general care as to well feeding and warmth. As medicine, give three grains of sulphate of copper (blue stone), finely powdered, every day for three or four days; then, when the mucus disappears a cure is nearly certain; yet care and special attention are requisite for a few days more, and it will be better if a grain of the sulphate be sprinkled with the bran every other day until the patient is perfectly restored to health. As this is a complaint of which many rabbits that are exposed to cold die, too much care cannot be exercised to prevent the attack, which will at times continue two or three weeks, especially in damp foggy weather. Carrots are beneficial at this time as part of the vegetable diet.

Sore Hocks.—Mr. T. C. Lord says that "for this there are two causes, viz., impurity and overheating of the blood, brought on chiefly from improper feeding, which causes a kind of boil or heat lump to appear, and the under part of the back legs being always in contact with the floor of the hutch, the disease generally shows itself in this place first; but I have known one instance where the boil appeared on the belly of the rabbit. The other cause arises from the hutch not being properly cleaned, and the rabbit having to stand in damp litter causes the leg to become tender, and in time the disease comes on. As prevention is always better than cure, I would advise all rabbit keepers to see that their hutches are at all times well cleaned out, and supplied with a good litter." Remedy: Apply some healing salve, to be procured of any druggist, and bandage the feet up. These bandages the animal will probably tear off, so that frequent renewal may be requisite. If the soreness is on the upper side of the foot, near the claws, there is less difficulty. Keep the rabbit warm and quiet, well supplied with nutritious food, and there is every probability of an ultimate cure.

Mr. Lord continues: "If the sore turns to suppuration, or, more plainly speaking, if it runs with matter, wash the place well with fresh water and a soft sponge till it is well cleaned out, then if there is any appearance of matter remaining put on a bread poultice to draw it out. After this is done anoint with 'fuller's earth,' and bandage the place well up. In the pollard, or morning meal, mix once or twice a week a small portion of sulphur, which will cool the blood, and at the same time cleanse the stomach. Give a moderate supply of dandelion or other green food."

Sores.—If the sore places assume the form of gatherings, which is the case at times, an application of the lancet in skilful hands may afford relief; then wash out all that is objectionable with warm water, and a cure will be effected in a short time.

Tape Worm.—Little requires to be said in reference to this rare appearance as one of the ills to which rabbits are liable, yet there are isolated cases when it will be found requisite to resort to the medicine chest. Remedy: 5 to 10 drops of oil of male fern given in a syrup twice a day for three days. This is not distasteful to the rabbits as a rule, for they have no serious objection to a little sugar in their milk and bread occasionally. After two or three days' attention as described, little trouble will be required afterwards.

Tumour.—The use of the lancet in skilful hands is an experiment worth the trial. Cases of tumour are by no means of frequent occurrence, and external applications, by way of fomentations, seem to produce no satisfactory results. Keep the rabbit warm, particularly after any surgical operation has been performed; feed well, and treat the case in its first stages, as the most favourable issue may then be hoped for.

Wax in Ears.—See under "Ear Gum."

CHAPTER VI.

SUMMARY.

1. Never allow any one to rush into the rabbitry.
2. Exclude all strange dogs.
3. Avoid entering the rabbitry about mid-day, because at that time the inmates are generally asleep, and prefer quiet.
4. Be as regular as possible in the times of feeding.
5. Be equally so as to the days for thorough cleaning.
6. When any offensive smell is perceived in any hutch, find out the cause, and apply a remedy.
7. Never allow any complaint or disease to be neglected, before restoratives are applied, for all ailments are more easily cured when treated at once.
8. Separate any diseased rabbit from the others as soon as discovered.
9. Do not hesitate to frequently "look over" your stock yourself.
10. Examine the noses, eyes, roots of ears, also the internal ear, to detect any appearance of scurf, mange, or ear gum, to which rabbits are liable in ill-ventilated hutches.
11. Let the air of the rabbitry be renewed as frequently as possible, to insure the health of inmates.
12. Keep the temperature of rabbitry as genial and equable as possible.
13. Always allow food to be seen in the feeding dish of suckling does, remembering that they require more nourishment during that time.
14. In proportion to the number of rabbits the doe has been suckling, so should the time be regulated for her pairing again.
15. If the litters are too frequent the stock will be weak. Quality and quantity are both important, but one must be subservient to the other.
16. Avoid handling young rabbits, especially when in the nests.
17. Exclude all mice from the hutches or rabbitry if possible,

for one mouse may cause the does to neglect many valuable young ones.

18. Never leave the rabbits to the care of inexperienced attendants; for one day's ignorance as to their wants may injure the stock, requiring many days of restoratives.

19. If rabbits are to be improved in condition, use little or no green food.

20. Never give any green food wet.

21. Cheap (so called) food is more expensive than that more nutritious and apparently dearer, as the most wholesome saves both the pocket and the rabbits, as six months' trial will prove.

22. Use as few artificial means as possible in the rearing and management of your rabbits.

23. Protect from a damp and foggy atmosphere as much as possible, as such is more injurious than a dry cold one.

24. Make a study of your rabbits, as to their habits and requirements, and experience will be gained in a few months which will enable you to become a successful "fancier;" and never forget that rabbits are not the objectionable creatures some persons would have you believe. In a well arranged rabbitry, where the health and comfort of both your rabbits and your friends is studied, you and they will be convinced that with proper care and attention, a large amount of pleasure may result from the hobby.

CHAPTER VII.

RABBITS AS A FOOD SUPPLY.

THE question, Can rabbits render any real service towards materially lessening the scarcity of animal food? may, I think, be answered in the affirmative to some extent; yet I should not expect to be able so to supply the market as to bring down the price of beef and mutton to that of former years. We all know that the numerous warrens in the United Kingdom send forth tons of rabbit flesh during the season; yet some of the rabbits are very small and weakly, by reason of the "in and in" breeding which has gone on for years; defects which an occasional interchange of stock would, to a certain extent, have obviated. If I were to advise what change to make as an improvement, I should suggest the introduction into the warrens of animals of a larger variety, after they have been reared to six or eight months old in a semi-wild state, or, at least, in hutches at a lower temperature than ordinary, by way of preparation for their life of exposure. Perhaps the most successful experiment would be to introduce the Belgian hare-rabbit, which is a large and handsome rabbit, 7lb. to 10lb. say (I have seen them a little heavier), and of a docile disposition. From the latter quality they would soon become on good terms with their newly-acquired companions. I think a few dozen of these "turned down" in a warren of ordinary dimensions would, in a couple of seasons, produce most satisfactory results, and though expensive at the first, would eventually return a fair percentage upon the original outlay.

The plan would be to procure half a dozen does and bucks ready to pair, and to allow the doe to have only four litters in the year, in order that the stock might be strong; thus, calculating for all casualties to which the young are liable from their birth to maturity, a goodly number would be ready the next season for "turning down." If this process were continued for a year or two each season, procuring, if possible, the breeding stock from other sources, the effect would be very evident in the increase of size of the progeny. The Belgian hare-rabbit may be kept for house use either in the hutch, or in a court in a semi-wild state. My experience proves that the larger varieties consume but very little more food than those not much more than half their size, and the larger varieties are undoubtedly the most remunerative in a commercial point of view. It may be said that the small varieties of common rabbits, tame or wild, are more prolific, and so, if smaller, they make up by numbers what they lack in size. This I rather question, as I have large Belgians which frequently bring forth from eight to eleven at a litter. I think the only way to fairly test the matter is to consider the cost of keeping, say 100 rabbits of the small size, and the same number of the kind I allude to; I think the difference in cost will be trivial, but the amount of food for the table just the reverse. I at times increase the size for the table by a careful crossing with a variety larger than the Belgian hare-rabbit.

Rabbits for ordinary purposes might be kept to advantage in far greater numbers than they are; and they would amply repay their keepers for the small amount of care they require, and the trifling cost of the food, by furnishing an agreeable and wholesome food at a cheap rate.

An authority says: "Rabbits are very profitable if properly managed, for there is no kind of herbage grown but what they will eat; even box and ivy clippings, which is poison to most animals, they will eat greedily. Sedge grass or weeds of any kind, which may be gathered from the sides of the road eight months in the year, and a few turnips, rabi or wurtzel, with dried weeds, leaves, and grass stored away in summer for winter use are sufficient, so that rabbits may be kept eight months in the year without any cost. They will breed five times a year, and average six at a litter, which will sell in the London markets at 1s. each, at twelve weeks old. The breeding does should be in pens, for if let to run loose they will fight, and in the scuffle kill the young. The young, when leaving the doe at five weeks, may run together until three months old, when the males must be cut, or they will fight and kill each other.

"It is a good plan to buy rabbits dropped early in the season, and keep them until February before breeding from them. Let them run together until then, afterwards place them in separate pens and keep them very quiet. The young ones when six weeks old may be taken from them. Leaves of any kind may be stored in an outhouse, trodden in tight and sprinkled with a little salt, and rabbits will live on them all through the winter with a mangold wurtzel or a carrot now and then. The most hardy for killing purposes are the Himalayan, the common wild colour, fawns or smuts."

I, however, think that if for the table, the Belgian hare-rabbits are the best, as they are large, soon arrive at maturity, are not difficult to rear to 8lb. or 10lb., and are ready for the table at six months, or earlier. Six or eight does to one buck will be about the number required as a breeding stock. If the does are procured when two or three months old they will all live together until eight or ten months, when required for pairing. The hutch should be not less than ten to twelve square feet, and the buck should occupy a separate hutch. My remarks upon feeding, hutches, &c., apply as much to rabbits for the table as for the show pen.

THE BELGIAN HARE RABBIT.

CHAPTER VIII.

A RABBIT COURT, AND HOW TO STOCK IT.

By T. C. LORD.

A "Rabbit Court" is a place adapted for breeding and rearing of such stock as is intended chiefly for the provision market as a source of profit; and, if properly managed, there can be little doubt that it is the best plan that could be thought of for the purpose.

In the first place select a courtyard, such as is generally seen in the rural districts, which must be well paved with flags or large-sized sets, to keep the animals from burrowing into the ground or making their way out under the walls. This court should be bounded on each side by a wall of at least 5ft. 6in. high, the higher the better, as rabbits, being very active and lithe of limb, are at times likely to make their escape over the wall if it be low enough for them to leap; and it is a well-known fact that some rabbits have an extraordinary power of leaping. If it is bounded on two of the sides by buildings, such as stabling or outhouses, so much the better, as besides preventing the rabbits from escaping, they will keep off the cold winds during the winter season. In selecting the courtyard, it is best to have one in which the sun shines freely during the summer months, and this is the chief season for breeding, and warmth is most essential in breeding for size. Perhaps the illustration marked Fig. 12 may be found useful in giving an easier explanation than words could do. A is the doorway leading in and out of the court; BB represents the does' hutches, which should be placed in in a row on each side, as shown in the illustration; CC are two

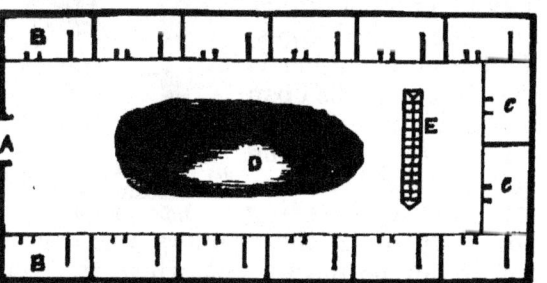

FIG. 12. PLAN OF RABBIT COURT.

A. Door into court; B. Does' hutches; C. Bucks' hutches; D. Mound of earth for burrows; E. Feeding trough.

hutches for the use of the bucks, which of course do not require the breeding compartment, represented in the does' hutches by a short mark near one side of each; and D is a large mound of earth in the centre, in which the rabbits will burrow during the daytime, but the keeper should be mindful that they do not sleep there

FIG. 13. WALL INSIDE COURT, WITH HUTCHES.

during the night, as in winter they are thus liable to be frozen to death. This mound will be found to have a great effect in keeping off the bad smell so often noticed in places where rabbits are kept; and I think it has a tendency to keep off the strong taste often found in rabbits kept in confinement. Fig. 13 is an illustration of one side of the court from the inside, showing the hutches, as placed side by side. Fig. 14 is a drawing of a hutch, which is simple in construction, easily managed, and cheap as regards cost. It is made out of one of those boxes used by provision dealers for the transit of bacon, and commonly known as "bacon boxes," and its first cost, before being made into a hutch is, I believe, about 1s. The wood of which it is made is about 1in. in thickness, and 3ft. 6in. long, by 2ft. 6in. wide; this is quite large enough for use in the rabbit court, as during fine weather (except when breeding) the rabbits will remain in the courtyard and burrows in the daytime, and merely take to the hutches at night when they want to rest. The door A is made so that it will let up and down instead of opening at the side with hinges, the reason of which is that it has to be open in the daytime for the rabbits to go in and out at their leisure. The door to breeding

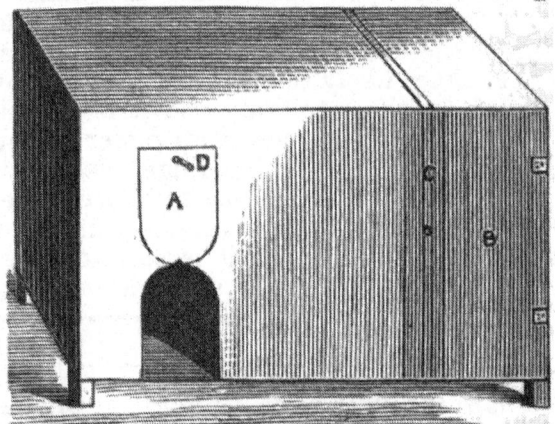

FIG. 14. RABBIT COURT HUTCH.
A. Door to ordinary compartment; B. Door to breeding box; C. Sliding partition; D. Peg to hold door up.

box B opens in the ordinary manner. C is a sliding partition, which can be drawn out when the young rabbits are about a month old, so that they may have more room to run about the hutch without hurting themselves. D is a peg which holds up the door when it has to be kept open. The feeding trough is an ordinary wooden one, bound at the edges with tin to prevent the rabbits from destroying it, and pieces of wire soldered across the top to keep them from scratching out the food.

The selection of stock is of the greatest importance and requires very careful attention. The silver-grey is well known as a hardy animal, but it does not attain the size that would be likely to produce a good sale as a source of meat supply; and, as this is the great end to aim at in breeding rabbits in this manner, I could not advise this variety. I have, however, known the silver-grey to be recommended on account of the value of its fur, which is said to command a good price amongst the fur dealers; but I do not think these would bring in a sufficient remuneration to the breeder in this country, for he would scarcely have a fair chance of competing with the breeders in France and other places on the Continent, as the articles for which the furs are required are chiefly manufactured in foreign countries. The Himalayan is not even so large as the silver-grey, and is scarcely so hardy. The common tame English prick-eared rabbit is better suited to this purpose than either of the above, from the fact of its being a more prolific breeder, and that it grows to a much larger size. The lop ear is known to gain a greater size than any of those before mentioned, the weight being sometimes as much as 15lb. or 16lb., and in one or two extreme cases has been known to be about 18lb.; but as this class is only suited for being kept in a place which is always at a temperature of not less than $50°$, its selection is almost out of the question; but I have known some good breeding does produce some very large young ones when kept in an outside hutch. The Patagonian, or, as it is sometimes improperly called, Andalusian or ram rabbit, would in my opinion be the best for selection, as it is in reality the largest in the whole variety. This rabbit is said to be as large at nine or ten weeks old as many of the other breeds are at four and five months.

The number of rabbits to be kept depends entirely on the size of the court; but to commence with about twelve or fifteen good breeding does are sufficient to produce a very large supply in a twelvemonth's time. It is a bad plan to have the court overstocked with breeders, for the simple reason that they may not always receive the proper amount of attention that a moderate stock would; and if rabbits are neglected it is of no use trying to keep them, as they are then liable at any time to be attacked with the infectious diseases these animals are subject to; and if this were to occur, a whole courtyardful might soon be carried off without the slightest chance of stopping the disease. Two good bucks will be quite sufficient for the above number of does, but I would advise a change every few months, as the relationship might get so intermingled that the rabbits would breed back.

It is absolutely necessary that the court should be well attended to and kept in a state of thorough cleanliness, as this and proper feeding is the secret of rabbits being kept in a sound, healthy condition; and as prevention is always better than cure, the wisest plan that can be adopted is to use every possible means in keeping back the diseases that are liable to break out in a rabbit court. The hutches should be cleaned out regularly once a week, and kept well supplied with good sweet hay or straw, during the winter season, as a kind of bedding for the rabbits. In summer I recommend the use of sawdust for bedding instead of straw or hay, as it is not so apt to become heated and breed fleas and other vermin, which are often very troublesome to rabbits during the hot season. The floor of the court should be well drained to prevent water from lodging in any part. If any of the rabbits should become infected with any disease, destroy them immediately, and thus stop the disease from spreading. It is not worth the labour of the keeper to attempt to cure the disease, as the loss of one or two animals would not very materially affect the profit account, and to allow diseased animals to remain amongst the others would in all probability cause a general epidemic, and thus produce a serious result.

The keeper of the court should adopt two different courses of feeding, one during the breeding season, and the other when the young rabbits are about ten or twelve weeks old, and are ready for fattening up for the market. For the first give in the morning, about seven or eight o'clock, barley meal and bran, pollard, or oatmeal and bran, mixed with warm water to a kind of mash or porridge; at dinner, about one o'clock, plenty of green food, such as endive, parsley, cabbage leaves, boiled potatoes, dandelion, carrots, celery tops, beetroot, parsnips, sow-thistles, fennel, &c.; about five or six o'clock in the evening, the same meal as in the morning, with the addition of good sweet hay or clover. When any of the does are suckling young ones they should be supplied (every morning for the first three weeks from the time of kindling) with a small quantity of milk and water mixed; this will cause the doe to give more milk, and the young ones to thrive better. Until they have arrived at the age before mentioned, the young ones should be fed chiefly on green food, with plenty of parsley and broom to prevent pot-belly. After this age their food should be changed, and grey peas soaked in water till they sprout substituted for the morning meal; at noon, boiled rice sweetened with sugar; and at supper, barley meal or oatmeal, with a little condiment added, and mixed with water. During the time of fattening they should be confined in separate places, as they fatten much quicker in this state than when running loose. A small quantity of linseed mixed with the barley meal occasionally will also be found beneficial. If the rules set down herein are adhered to, I feel confident no complaint will be made as to the success of the undertaking.

ADVERTISEMENTS.

BOOKS PUBLISHED BY HORACE COX,
AT 346, STRAND, W.C.

THE IDSTONE PAPERS.—A Series of Articles and Desultory Observations on Sport and Things in General, written originally for *The Field* newspaper. Large post 8vo., price 7s. 6d.

THE DIAMOND DIGGINGS of SOUTH AFRICA.—A Personal and Practical Account. By "SARCELLE," of *The Field*. With a Brief Notice of the New Gold Fields. With Map, large post 8vo., price 6s.

ROUND the TABLE; or, Notes on Cookery and Plain Recipes, with a Selection of Bills of Fare. By "The G. C." All its recipes have been tested by experience, and are so given as to be intelligible of themselves, the object being not so much to provide a volume of reference for a professed cook as to explain how, with ordinary resources, an artistic dinner can be produced. Post 8vo., price 6s.

SECOND EDITION of the DOGS of the BRITISH ISLANDS. Edited by "STONEHENGE." Greatly enlarged (including new Parts on "Kennel Management of Dogs," and "Judging at Dog Shows and Field Trials"). 4to., gilt edges, toned paper, price 10s. 6d.

THE SILKWORM BOOK; or, Silkworms Ancient and Modern, their Food and Mode of Management. In demy 8vo., price 2s. 6d., cloth gilt; post free, 2s. 8d.

THE RURAL ALMANAC and SPORTSMAN'S ILLUSTRATED CALENDAR for 1873. Price 1s.; by post, 1s. 2d. [*Nearly ready.*

THE ANGLER'S DIARY, wherein the Angler can Register his Take of Fish throughout the Year. An extensive List of Fishing Stations throughout the World is added. In cloth, post 8vo., price 1s. 6d., post free 1s. 8d.

THE SHOOTER'S DIARY for 1872-73 contains Forms for Registering Game killed during the Year, either by a Single Gun or by a Party, or off the whole Estate. A List of Shooting Stations throughout the World is also given. Post 4to., price 1s. 6d.; post free 2d. extra.

FACTS and USEFUL HINTS relating to FISHING and SHOOTING, Illustrated; being a Collection of Information and Recipes of the greatest utility to the general Sportsman, to which is added a Series of Recipes on the Management of Dogs in Health and Disease. Second Edition, enlarged and revised. Large post 8vo., price 5s. cloth.

THE COUNTRY HOUSE; a Collection of Useful Information and Recipes of the greatest utility to the housekeeper generally. Illustrated. Second Edition, enlarged and revised. Large post 8vo., price 5s. cloth.

THE FARM: being Part I. of the Second Edition of the FARM, GARDEN, STABLE, and AVIARY. Valuable to country gentlemen, farmers, &c. Large post 8vo., price 5s.

THE GARDEN: being Part II. of the Second Edition of the FARM, GARDEN, STABLE, and AVIARY. Large post 8vo., price 5s.

THE STABLE: being Part III. of the Second Edition of the FARM, GARDEN, STABLE, and AVIARY. Large post 8vo., price 5s.

The Bazaar,
The Exchange and Mart,
and
Journal of the Household.

ILLUSTRATED.

EVERY WEEK: PRICE TWOPENCE.

GENERAL CONTENTS.

THE DRAWING ROOM.—Résumés of Dramatic, Art, Scientific, and Musical news of the week; Critiques on New Music; Articles on Art Subjects, &c., &c.

THE HALL.—Articles upon Canaries and all other Cage Birds; British Seaweeds; Management of Pets; Notes on Places at Home and Abroad; Miscellaneous Articles upon Subjects of General Interest.

THE LIBRARY.—Articles upon the Noteworthy Books recently published; Notes upon Various Literary Subjects.

THE WORKSHOP.—Articles and Notes upon Various Branches of Amateur Mechanics.

THE HOUSEKEEPER'S ROOM.—Articles upon Domestic Matters, Recipes of all kinds, &c.

THE BOUDOIR.—Notes on Present Fashions; Honiton Lace making; Fancy Work of different kinds.

THE GARDEN.—Articles upon the Cultivation of Flowers, Fruit, and Vegetables; British Ferns; Garden Operations; Bee Keeping, &c.

THE CURTILAGE.—Articles on Diseases of Dogs; Exhibition Rabbits; Farming; Poultry; Pigeons; Reports of Poultry, Pigeon, and Rabbit Shows.

COMING EVENTS.—Notice of the dates of all coming Public Concerts, Exhibitions, Sporting Contests, &c.

EXCHANGE AND MART.—Thousands of Articles of *every* description for Exchange, or Sale, or Wanted by *private persons*.

WANTS AND VACANCIES.—Governesses, Tutors, Clerks, Servants, and others Wanting Situations, and Situations Vacant.

Quarterly Subscription, 2s. 8d., post paid.

May be had at the Railway Bookstalls, and from all Respectable Newsagents.

LONDON OFFICE: 32, WELLINGTON-STREET, STRAND, W.C.

Rabbits For Prizes and Profit.

PART III.

EXHIBITION RABBITS.
PART I.

By CHARLES RAYSON.

ILLUSTRATED.

LONDON:
"THE BAZAAR" OFFICE, 32, WELLINGTON-STREET,
STRAND, W.C.

PRICE SIXPENCE.

ADVERTISEMENTS.

LOPS.—The undersigned Amateur has a small Stock from the best Prize strains, and will be glad to SELL or EXCHANGE from time to time.—Address T. COMPTON, Esq., Winscombe, near Weston-super-Mare.

THE ART of PYROTECHNY: Being Comprehensive and Practical Instructions for the MANUFACTURE of FIREWORKS, specially designed for the use of Amateurs. Illustrated. By W. H. BROWNE, Ph.D., M.A., L.R.C.P., &c. Large post 8vo., in parts, price 6d., by post 6½d. each.

WORKING IN SHEET METAL: being practical instruction for making and mending small Articles in Tin, Copper, Iron, Zinc, and Brass. Illustrated. Large post 8vo., price 6d., by post 6½d.

PRACTICAL BEE-KEEPING: Being Plain Instructions to the Amateur for the Successful Management of the Honey Bee. Illustrated. Large post 8vo., price 6d., by post 6½d.

TURNING for AMATEURS, containing full description of the lathe, with all its working parts and attachments, and minute instructions for the effective use of them on wood, metal, and ivory. Illustrated with 129 first-class wood engravings. Large post 8vo., cloth, price 2s. 6d., by post 2s. 9d.

BRITISH MARINE ALGÆ: Being a Popular Account of the SEAWEEDS of GREAT BRITAIN, their Collection and Preservation. By W. H. GRATTANN. In parts, large post 8vo., price 6d., by post 6½d. each.

HONITON LACE MAKING, containing plain, practical instructions for the making of this beautiful pillow lace. Beautifully Illustrated. Large post 8vo., price 1s., by post 1s. 1d.

THE DISEASES OF DOGS: their Pathology, Diagnosis, and Treatment. To which is added a complete Dictionary of Canine Materia Medica. By HUGH DALZIEL. Large post 8vo., price 1s., by post 1s. 1d.

BREEDING POULTRY for PRIZES—Being full directions for the proper selection of stock birds, the points required, &c., for the successful production of prize poultry, and numerous first-class wood engravings of fowls and feathers, showing the shapes and markings that must be aimed at. By JAMES LONG (winner of the New York Poultry Society's Prize for the best "Thesis on the Breeding and Management of Poultry.") THIRD EDITION. Large post 8vo., price 6d., by post 6½d.

EXHIBITION POULTRY (Part I.)—Being minute and accurate descriptions of Cochins, Dorkings, Spanish, Brahmas, French Fowl, Game, and their varieties, such as they must be to entitle them to success in the show pen. By JAMES LONG. Illustrated with four full-page portraits of prize birds. SECOND EDITION. Large post 8vo., price 6d., by post 6½d.

EXHIBITION POULTRY (Part II.)—Being minute and accurate descriptions of Hamburghs, Polands, Malays, Bantams, "Any other Varieties," and Turkeys, such as they must be to entitle them to success in the show pen. By JAMES LONG. Illustrated with four full-page portraits of prize winners. Large post 8vo., price 6d., by post 6½d.

"THE BAZAAR" OFFICE, 32, WELLINGTON STREET, STRAND, W.C.

CHAPTER IX.

THE ANGORA.

(For illustration see Frontispiece.)

THE Angora, originally from the town of that name in Asia Minor, but now spread far and wide over the continent of Europe, is sometimes called the French and Russian rabbit, yet it is different from these, both as regards general appearance and the silky fineness of its wool, that of the true-bred Angora being long and approaching to a curl, and so exceedingly soft and fine in texture, that it becomes of commercial importance on the Continent. The Angora is exceedingly docile, and the buck is not always so fretful at his separation from the doe as sometimes represented, but it is wiser not to allow him to remain in the hutch with the young at the time of birth; for though he would not, in all probability, destroy them in the same ferocious manner as some males of other varieties, yet they would be in jeopardy, and perhaps be trampled to death. When inconvenienced for want of an extra hutch I have allowed the buck and doe to occupy the same up to within a week or ten days of the expected birth of the young ones.

This variety is prolific, from six to ten being the general number in each litter, but exhibition does should not be frequently littering, as they spoil their appearance by pulling off their fur to form their nests; they are, as a rule, affectionate and kind to their offspring and very tractable as pets. When the young are eight weeks old they can be removed from the mother, but they should not be placed in too small a hutch, or too many together, for, if they are, their wool will become matted, and the next moult, with the assistance of a metal comb, will alone remove the unsightly lumps and knots. If the wool of the Angora does not become matted from neglect the animal is not of that pure, silky, long-wooled variety so essential in a good specimen; to keep the wool in order is by no means a great difficulty, for an occasional combing by way of assisting nature in the process of moulting is all that is required. The showy appearance depends to a great extent upon the manner in which the wool is kept.

The ears are generally rather short and erect, but they vary a little in this respect. The colour most "fashionable" is the pure white, as it probably best tends to display the rich fullness of the wool, yet it by no means follows that white alone will insure a prize at a show, for a variety of shades, such as black, grey, fawn, and slate, as self colours, and black and white, grey and white sometimes receive first prizes. The most important points are the size and form of the animal with the all-important fineness and length of wool, irrespective of marking of colour, and if exhibitors would pay a little more attention to their specimens in the way of "dressing" for the exhibition, they would find it to their advantage.

It is interesting to notice the variety of marking the progeny will present with judicious care in pairing, as, for instance, with a white buck and grey doe, or white doe and black and white buck, and as the colour of this variety is not so uniform as that of the Himalayan, or some other kinds, a little experimenting in the production of diversity in colours may be indulged in.

CHAPTER X.

THE BELGIAN HARE-RABBIT.

(For illustration see page 48.)

This fine large specimen of the rabbit family is now much more cared for than when first imported into this country, when its real value for culinary purposes was almost unknown. It is, in many instances, as large as the hare, weighing from 7lb. to 10lb., and bears a strong resemblance to that animal in many respects, as, for instance, in the shade of its fur, which is almost of the same deep sandy tinge, though not quite so long and regular in growth as that of the hare, but more even and smooth like some of the other short-haired varieties of rabbits. It is generally imported from Belgium, yet good specimens are also found in France and other continental countries, but they are only reared in small quantities, and the best specimens are from Belgium.

It was for a time supposed that this useful variety was a hybrid between the hare and rabbit, but this is clearly proved not to be the case; it is merely designated "hare-rabbit," on account of its strong resemblance to the hare; in its habits, feeding and other peculiarities, it is allied to the rabbit. This kind will live to advantage upon the ground when turned down for breeding at six or eight months old, if some protection be afforded against the vicissitudes of the climate, and thus in two or three generations a valuable, hardy stock may be reared at small cost, for their size will always render them vastly superior to the small warren varieties, which by the continued "in and in" breeding are often less healthy and very diminutive. When a dozen or more pairs of this large variety are introduced into a warren, the result is, as may be supposed, very satisfactory. However, as I purpose to speak of rabbits in hutches more than in a semi-wild state, I shall treat the Belgian as a fancy variety, irrespective of its worth as an article of food.

Injudicious crossings of this variety are often resorted to, which answer no beneficial purpose, so that some so-called hare-rabbits appear but one remove from the common grey hutch rabbit, devoid of that true hare-like shade of fur, and with ears much shorter than the pure-bred specimen, the ears of which should be about 5¼ inches in length and proportionately broad, so that this rabbit may be said to have rather a large ear, yet they will vary a little in this point; they are at times inclined to hang over, as if too long to remain erect. The pendulous position of the ear is not frequent with a good specimen; but the ears present more of the hare-like size and shape, except that they do not incline backwards, as in the hare. The body of the Belgian is longer in proportion than in any other kind of equal weight, and it is not always of that beautiful outline which is a point of excellence in some rabbits, such, for instance, as the lop. A "dew lap," of tolerable proportion, is found in some of the larger specimens, giving them somewhat the appearance of the lop-eared variety in this particular, but not many are found with this soft appendage. The head is in due proportion to the size, rather broad across the eyes, and tapering off towards the nose in gradual outline; somewhat long from root of ears to tip of nose, yet all in proportion, and imparting to the general appearance a sort of easy, good-natured look; a little white will be found under the body, but if this does not extend too far up the sides, it may not be deemed objectionable, even for an exhibition specimen. The points to be aimed at are first true hare-like shade of fur, and that as general as possible over the body; and then size, the larger the better, providing all other essentials are present; all white streaks on the face, or white feet are objectionable for prize specimens.

They vary like most other kinds in the care they manifest towards their young, yet the does are generally possessed of strong maternal regard, and though frequently from seven to eleven are found in each litter, it is seldom that any of them die during the time they remain in the nest. They are probably more easily startled than some varieties; a loud peal of thunder, or the presence of a mouse in the hutch, or any sudden shock, will often cause them to neglect their young; yet some specimens are equally confident and fearless, and will sometimes make their nests directly opposite the doors of the hutch, leaving the comfortably dark corner, usually resorted to, unnoticed. They are very docile, and not so pugnacious as some of the smaller varieties, and they do not consume as much food as might be supposed from their size; they are by no means fastidious, eating almost anything with a relish.

Their hutches should be at least five feet by two feet, and as much more as convenient, to insure their health, and an occasional run on the ground or dry grass for an hour will be of service to them; in fact, this should be allowed to all rabbits, usually confined in small hutches, at least once or twice a week, providing the ground is dry and warm, and whilst this treat is afforded the hutch can be cleaned and purified by the free admission of fresh air. The Belgian, though not so showy as some of the other varieties, by reason of its self colour, is still a noble looking animal; and, for domestic use, probably of greater value than any of its more externally attractive companions in the rabbitry, as it will lie in outside hutches all the year round, or in a semi-wild state upon the ground; it is hardy, and few are born but what may, with ordinary care and attention, be reared to maturity. Perhaps to regard it as a rabbit of great utility rather than as a mere pet is more satisfactory; yet, as a variety, it is decidedly an acquisition to any rabbitry.

In general management it requires no deviation from the plan adopted in reference to other kinds, except, perhaps, that a lower degree of temperature will do for the hutch (or if a large room all the better) than that found requisite for some more delicate varieties; its skin, when properly cured, is worth preserving, as it is large and may be serviceable for many domestic purposes.

CHAPTER XI.

THE HIMALAYAN RABBIT.

ALTHOUGH this neat animal is *said* to be found in great numbers on the chain of mountains from which it takes it name (the meaning of which is "a palace of snow"), which extends 1800 miles from Brahmapootra, in Assam, to the western extremity of the Hindoo-Koosh, in Cabul, the popular idea has no foundation in fact. It is asserted to be a sacrificial rabbit with the Chinese, who are said to annually offer up 30,000 upon 1600 altars, with prayers that the crops and fruits generally may be as prolific as rabbits. Be this as it may, the rabbit is frequently spoken of as "Chinese," also "black-nosed rabbit from China," and was so labelled, I believe in the Zoological Gardens when first introduced into this country. They seem to luxuriate in many names, such as Egyptian Smut, Polish rabbit, and I have seen them entered at exhibitions as Antwerp rabbits; this undoubtedly was because of many having been brought from that city, where they were, and are probably still reared in great numbers.

As a rule they breed very true to colour, but sometimes an irregularity and want of decision in the marking will be observable even amongst a litter from pure prize winning stock (such, for example, as a grey tip approaching to whiteness half an inch long upon one foot), though this is of rare occurrence; but this is one of the drawbacks connected with even the most successful rearing of rabbits, and one to which all varieties are liable; it demonstrates the fact that the most perfect animals will not always produce offspring of equal merit.

In this variety there should be as perfect an uniformity in the shade of dark points as possible, the darker the better, the best being almost approaching to blackness. The nose and ears are generally of the right shade, but the front feet are often a little lighter, and the hinder still more grey, in fact, the feet often prevent the rabbit from being found in a first position at an exhibition; it is seldom that the ears (which should be rather short and erect) and nose present the objectionable grey shade, except when

THE HIMALAYAN RABBIT.

the animal is moulting; and, when such is the case, it is not in a fit condition for exhibition. The eye presents a peculiar and beautiful pink shade, especially if seen in a certain light. There is a smart neatness about the Himalayan, that must ever make it attractive; it possesses an amount of courage that will always protect it from being overcome by an inferior power; but it is of an affectionate disposition, tending with great care its young—generally from five to eight at a birth—and watching with a jealous eye any movement of the hand that dares to intrude within the precincts of the nest, which will be found at the remote corner of the hutch.

When the young have left their nests, and are from three to four weeks old, little of the necessary dark tinge is evident; perhaps to an inexperienced eye they will appear to be pure white rabbits, yet close observation will detect the dark shade on the ears and nose especially, and, in a little time, the feet also will assume the same desirable shade, and, at five months, some of the young will appear almost fully developed in this particular, whilst others will require a few weeks more before being fit to exhibit. I have seen them exhibited at four or five months, with a fine rich shade upon nose and ears, yet generally from six to eight months are requisite to perfect this great essential for successful competition. Should the ears require longer time than the nose, or even the feet, which occurs in some instances, let the owner not be disappointed, for this will be the case frequently, and when all but the ears are almost in a state of perfection, they should be allowed a few extra weeks before they are pronounced against.

Little advantage can result from crossing this variety with others, as the more perfect each specimen is in the essential particulars, the better for satisfactory results. I have for my own satisfaction and for experience paired a well-marked doe with a Polish buck, and in six or seven generations have obtained tolerably well marked specimens, but this experiment was of no real advantage, except for the knowledge derived, which may be of use to others.

I had my first Himalayans brought from the East; some died on the voyage, but others I was so fortunate as to keep alive, and I have reared from this stock many which I now have in my rabbitry. They are not a large rabbit, weighing generally from four to six pounds. I have known them heavier, but this is rare, and, when seen, it will be generally found that they are not quite so dark in points as the smaller ones, but if large, well proportioned, and with the indispensable dark points also, they are valuable.

They require tolerable warmth, and are best kept in inside hutches, yet they are by no means a difficult variety to rear with the usual care, and, as a rule, they are more speedily restored to health than other varieties, and more free, also, from the many complaints to which rabbits kept in an artificial manner are liable. The fur is valuable and may be used for many purposes, it is sometimes called "mock ermine," as it is finer and more lustrous than that of the common white animal, and on the Continent in particular it is considered of importance.

Chloride of lime should not be used as a disinfectant in the hutch of this variety (the less the better in any, for it is liable to affect the feet) as it destroys the shade of the fur—so all important.

CHAPTER XII.

THE DUTCH RABBIT.

(For illustration see page 30.)

THIS pretty variety of fancy pet, which may be considered the very "dwarf" of the rabbit family, is undoubtedly originally from Holland, where it is reared in large numbers; it is also found in France, where it is named Nicard. It is much valued in Old Provence, and in this country there are but few rabbitries with a varied stock which do not include some specimens. It is not, by reason of its size, of the same value as its larger neighbours, when reared for domestic purposes, yet many are used for the table, and are preferred by some to the larger varieties.

The points are, body of any self colour, such as black, grey, blue (or slate), lemon, and tortoiseshell (the last is the most valuable, as it is not frequently found); a white ring round the neck, which should be of equal width and collar-like, a white streak up the face, which is better if tapering off towards the crown, each foot tipped with white from three-quarters of an inch or over the claws to near the first joint in the leg, the more uniform the better in this respect, but frequently the fore legs will present the greatest length of such white marking, so that it will appear connected with the white portion of the collar; it is all the better if distinct from it, as it renders the white tips of the feet more conspicuous. Out of several litters not many may have all these valuable points, although well-marked stock for pairing is more likely to produce satisfactory results, yet specimens with not much pretension to correctness of marking will at times produce valuable stock, frequently equal to exhibition standard. I have tried many experiments in this particular, and with an almost perfect blue buck, and one of the most imperfectly marked does, being almost all white, or faint patches of lemon colour spread over the body, and with little appearance of belonging to the Dutch family at all; out of six young ones in the litter, two were quite as perfect and fit for exhibition as the buck; all except one were blue as the sire. There seems less certainty as to the result with this kind than with some other varieties after careful pairing.

The does are excellent mothers, and are by nature, one would almost suppose, intended to supply the deficiency of others in the rabbitry, as they will rear many not belonging to them, and as nurses are of great use; when therefore a more valuable specimen seems over-burdened with too large a family, the little Dutch will be found an excellent foster mother, for she seems more anxious about the quantity of good food with which she is supplied than the number of young ones placed under her care. They are exceedingly affectionate and docile, yet by no means cowardly, and I have seen a specimen three pounds in weight make a bold attack upon a fourteen pound Patagonian; yet they are not generally pugnacious, but only defend their rights when such are in danger. They evince great affection for their young, tending them with much care and seem very confident in those around them.

I have had does arrive at my rabbitry during the last few days of their gestation, that had come over closely packed from Holland, and so weak for want of food and overcrowding in the basket, that some of them have had young two days after their arrival, when so feeble as to be unable to prepare a nest (about which they are very particular), and the young ones have been scattered about the hutch, yet after a few days' rest, and good feeding, they have then commenced the process of nest making around their little families, which had been collected together for them in a suitable corner of the hutch, and, when their strength was restored, have tended them with that maternal care so peculiar to their nature.

In this variety the "in and in" breeding is resorted to for diminution of size, and I have heard of specimens not more than one and half pounds in weight. It must always be considered that such diminution of size by this process also implies weakness of body, and that hardy vigorous nature peculiar to this variety is decidedly interfered with by such means. I have seen specimens from Holland from four to five pounds weight, but it is probably seldom that any are found at exhibitions but what have been born in this country.

The doe will rarely produce more than from five to eight in each litter; the mode of treatment is the same as for other fancy hutch varieties, they require to be kept free from cold and damp, yet fresh air is essential to ensure strength and health. To say which is the greatest favourite with fanciers would be difficult, for all have their tastes in respect to marking, shade, &c. The greatest contrast is undoubtedly evident in the black-bodied animal, and least in the lemon, with its white collar and feet; there seems almost as great a diversity of colour in this as some of the larger varieties, as Angoras or lops, each and all being more or less attractive, as fancy dictates.

THE LOP-EAR.

CHAPTER XIII.

THE LOP-EAR.

THERE are, probably, in this valuable and graceful variety more distinctive points to be observed than in any other. The almost fabulous price which a perfect specimen will fetch seems extraordinary; I have seen more than one for which £20 have been given, although in these instances, in addition to being perfect specimens, a reputation for prize winning may have enhanced their importance. The diversity of colour found in the lop affords ample gratification for all tastes, but, for a certain length of time, one shade of marking seems more in request or fashionable than another, although most exhibitions now give a separate class for each colour. There are probably more disputes with regard to the lop than about any other kind in reference to the varied points, especially in regard to the vexed but all-important question, length of ears; the prize, however, is not always awarded at exhibitions to the longest-eared rabbit, but for the best, all properties considered—so that the process of ear-stretching need no longer be inhumanly resorted to.

The points generally considered necessary, and which are, with slight deviations, adopted in the code of rules by most of the clubs, are as follows: First, length of ear; Secondly, width; Thirdly, position of the ear, which should fall behind the inner corner of the eye in a graceful manner, and as close to the cheek as possible, with the convex surface outwards; it should be of same colour as the prevailing one of the body; towards the root it should be narrow and thick, and rather abruptly becoming broader and proportionately thinner towards the tip—for the fineness of ear bespeaks to some extent the careful breeding—and when flexible and soft all the better; Fourthly, general colour (any shade) and uniformity of marking; Fifthly, the eye, which should be round and full, the larger the better if of proportionate shape; Sixthly, the general carriage, which should be rather low at the shoulders, and higher at the hind quarters, and with a dewlap upon which the head rests when in a state of repose; Seventhly, the size of the rabbit, which is of great importance. It is rare for one animal to possess all these points in perfection; yet some fair proportion of them must be present to secure an honourable position in any show.

There was a time when the "sooty fawn" was an immense favourite, although perhaps not quite so attractive in appearance as others of more decided contrast in shade. Probably the well-marked tortoiseshell is as valuable as most, or the grey and white, black and white, blue and white, yellow and white, and the self-coloured, as grey, fawn, black, and white, though the latter is more scarce than any of the others named. Although the requisite points of marking vary in the estimation of different fanciers, yet certain it is that there must be some peculiarity in the marking of the fur, irrespective of all other points requisite to the general "make-up." The following may, as a general rule, be accepted as some of the leading features in this particular:—The nose should have a dark spot on each side, being often of the same shade as the general marking of the body; a dark shade should run up the nose, meeting these two spots, thus forming a "butterfly smut" so designated because of a supposed resemblance to that insect. Around the eyes should be a colouring joining the ears upon the shoulders. The line or chain of equally spread spots should be uniform on each side, extending to the large patch of self-colour spreading over the body; the more free these and the other markings are from any sprinkling of differently-coloured hairs the better. The so-called saddle is of importance as to its bright clearness, let the colour be what it may, for this gives the name to the rabbit; as, if of yellow, it is said to be yellow and white; if black, then it is a black and white, and so on through the other colours.

With all the care possible in the selecting of almost perfect parents, in a litter of six or eight only one or two may present the same excellences; for in this there is by no means the same certainty of obtaining perfect specimens in the litters as may reasonably be expected in some other varieties, as the Himalayan, for instance. These remarks apply more particularly to those animals of varied colours, for the self-coloured varieties, when carefully paired with their own shades, will produce offspring with little deviation from what was expected.

In the all-important item of breeding and rearing lops, I am beset with a formidable array of opinions, as varied as the markings of the animal itself. In addition to my opinion and experience of many years, in this particular, as to—first, selection of stock, secondly, temperature in which they are born, and, thirdly, the rearing in general, which may all be worthy of notice, I have the opinions of some of the most successful breeders, metropolitan and provincial, some of whom are of many years' experience, which alone can render opinions valuable. Some well-known exhibitors and prize receivers probably never bred a really good lop in their lives, but they have purchased their valuable stock from well-known and successful breeders, who seldom, it may be, exhibit, yet to whom greater merit is due than to the mere purchaser for exhibition purposes.

Stock should be as perfect as possible in all respects; the parents should be large, the doe with ears from 19in., and buck from 21in. or 22in. and upwards—the longer the better; and the doe, if of a broken colour and paired with a sooty fawn buck, will produce some good specimens, from which, in their turn, promising animals may be bred. In fact, almost any colour may be obtained with a little study in crossing and re-crossing, as is the case with all other varieties, avoiding as much as possible close relationship, for colour alone can be gained by such injudicious pairing; and although such desirable marking may be the result, yet the stock will be found more weakly. Care must always be taken that rabbits are not mated with others of the same blood, hence the frequent change of sires to insure a stock being hardy and strong is very desirable.

Most breeders have their own opinions concerning the proper heat or temperature; but as now "best for all properties," is considered in most prize schedules, better rabbits are bred than years ago, when the longest-eared specimen, irrespective of other general properties, carried all before it. Then by any means length of ear had to be obtained, and many were the ingenious contrivances for securing the requisite length; many a specimen has obtained its immense size of ears by an application of artificial heat which has tended to shorten its life.

In order to secure the greatest length and breadth of ear, a small and warm hutch is better than a larger one, requiring a higher artificial heat than from 65 deg. to 70 deg., for at that heat the constitution will not be impaired. As some of these rabbits are treated in such a manner that their long ears mean short lives, the purchaser requires to exercise much caution in ascertaining how any new acquisition to his stock has been reared; for it is often found that a rabbit, after its removal to a new home, with a change of temperature, and often with different treatment, becomes sickly and dies.

Many other points of excellence are requisite to constitute a good lop besides length of ear; and though, when many points are necessary, it may require a year or two more to breed up to the highest standard than to obtain one point alone, nevertheless, from a money point of view, it is far wiser to rear the "good all round" animal; for the long-lived rabbit for stock purposes must, apart from exhibitions, be far more valuable than the other. Upon this I am anxious to express my opinion most fully, having received so many letters from those anxious to learn what my ideas are on this subject, and I say it is better to breed a good, healthy, all-property rabbit by fair means or moderate natural temperature, than a sickly one with only *one* property—immense ears—by artificial means. Of course, in a damp season, or damp rabbitry, it may be found requisite to introduce some little artificial heat to counteract the ill effects of the moisture so fatal to hutch rabbits in general, and lops in particular. A dry rabbitry, though rather cold, is less objectionable than a damp one, with all the appliances employed to obviate it; of course it is understood that the lop is decidedly an indoor variety, and its hutch is therefore more easily rendered comfortable. In my own rabbitry, a square building, containing from fifty to sixty specimens of six of the more delicate kinds, a gas burner is suspended from the centre of the roof at an equal distance from all the hutches, which are arranged on three sides; and this gaslight is allowed to burn an hour or two in early morning and late at night, or at any time when the damp prevails or the temperature is very low, but a convenient ventilator carries off all the deleterious effects of the combustion.

In rearing lops, little divergence need be made from the usual mode adopted. Give a liberal supply of warm bread and milk at least once a day to does just littering, especially in winter. It is better to breed this variety in summer, so as to insure greater success; those born in outside hutches should remain there, say, from March, when born, to October, and when 7 months old, they can be removed into the inner rabbitry, to be ready for breeding purposes in February or March; by this method they are strong and hardy, and better able to perform the duties of mothers. The does should not be burdened with too many young in the nest; two or three, particularly if they are intended to be "extra good," are enough. Perhaps no better foster-mothers can be found than the little Dutch, as they have abundance of milk, are affectionate, and not very particular as to the number under their care. Plenty of food must be given them, and to all does, during this time, and it should be of the most nutritious kind. In looking over the litter two or three days after the young are born, and selecting the best marked, or with the most promising ear (about which some idea may be formed at that early age), leave the best with the doe. If it be her first litter let two or three remain, and if she prove a good mother, then one or two more may be left next litter; that will however depend upon what they are intended for. I consider that the milk of the natural mother produces far healthier animals than that of a foster parent. Should no Dutch doe be kept; any good mother of a common kind will supply the requisite care, but in a rabbitry with some twenty-five or thirty does, it is always convenient to have four or five does littering at the same time, so that the number with each may be equalised—as some does will have only four or five, others twice the number, at each litter, and yet all be good mothers, with abundance of milk.

When the young ones are some ten or twelve weeks old, the ears may be taken between the thumb and forefinger and worked gently into position. If this be performed before a fire the result will be more satisfactory, particularly if it be cold weather; and it will soon be found that the ears assume a graceful form. The operation will be painful if continued for more than a minute or two at a time, although it may be repeated daily if of shorter duration. This tends also to expand the ear and develop it, and an addition from half to an inch may be gained by such treatment.

Amongst the best and most perfect litters, will be some rabbits whose ears have a tendency to fall otherwise than in the desired manner; some may have an oar-like appearance, *i.e.*, being in an horizontal position, and at right angles to the head, as if they were too strong and thick at the root to assume the graceful pendent position so important, others present the appearance of a pair of horns projecting in front of the head. Of the two the "oar-lop" is probably the less objectionable in appearance, yet even this is not fit for exhibition purposes. It is not, however, always desirable to discard an otherwise perfect rabbit from the stock hutch because of this one defect, for, with judicious care in pairing, some good specimens may be found amongst its offspring; but if, in addition to this important imperfection, others are presented, then to fatten for the table would be the wiser plan; or, if it be a large specimen, its possible success at an exhibition in a class for weight, might be a reason for retaining it, for as weight is the one point, any imperfections in marking, form of ears, &c., would be of no importance. The "half-lop" is another unsatisfactory appearance — where one ear falls in the proper way close to the cheek, while the other, obstinately refusing to follow its example, remains erect, giving an odd, undecided look. These imperfections of "side lops," "oar lop," "horn lop," and "half lop," may be, in many instances, removed or lessened if manipulated in time. The most satisfactory plan is to have a cap of leather with holes through which the ears may be placed, and if made of thin leather it may be tied under the chin, so as not to interfere with the comfort of the animal when eating. Another kind of cap can be made of thicker leather, so that when bent to the proper form towards the cheek it will remain so, requiring no string; the cap may continue a week or ten days in use, and all rabbits so treated should be alone, or both string and leather will at times be partially eaten by the others. Sticking the ears together with wax, and even stitching is a plan adopted, but these cruel practices will never be resorted to by those who have any kindly feeling towards their pets. If the rabbits be of the right kind, it is rare that any of these appliances are required, for the simple process of working the ears between the thumb and fingers as before mentioned is generally all that is requisite, but when other means are required, the cap is the most effective and humane.

Before concluding my remarks, I give the experience of some of the most successful breeders, who are more particularly celebrated for the valuable specimens reared in their rabbitries—some having had forty years' experience, and others half that time. Mr. Lock (London) says: "I never use any artificial heat except a gaslight during damp weather to produce a more genial heat, and never the high temperature of 70deg. or 80deg., which must tend to destroy the constitution of the rabbit. I do not adopt the high feeding that some do, but prefer to breed a good all-property rabbit by fair means. As regards pairing, I prefer a self-coloured buck with broken-coloured doe—a good sooty fawn buck, as from him with care you may obtain such a variety of colours." Mr. C. King (London) says: "I like a doe with ears from 19in. to 20in., and buck with ears as long as you can procure them, and from these some valuable specimens may be produced. Good lops may be reared to greater perfection in summer than winter, as less artificial heat is required. The doe should not bring up all her young ones if they are intended to be very good for exhibition purposes. This variety should have greater heat than some of the others, but not so high a temperature as to weaken them." Mr. J. Quick (London) says: "My plan is a very simple one with my lops; I procure the best I can, and feed them regularly with good food, keep them as near to about 60deg. as possible; and if cold weather, give them a warm feed in the evening of scalded barley meal, oats, and peas, &c. As regards the breeding, by working self colours you are sure to obtain good specimens of the same. My sooties were bred in that manner." Mr. A. H. Easten (Hull) says: "The parents should be as perfect as possible; the ears of the doe need be only 20in., provided there is good blood in her veins, and she is from a long-eared stock, but the buck must be as long as possible in the ears. With reference to heat, I at one time kept them in a high temperature of 85 deg. to 90 deg. by means of a stove kept burning all night; but this I found made the air too hot and dry, and there was an escape of sulphur injurious to them. I now rear all my rabbits in smaller hutches, kept dry and warm, and at a temperature of some 60 deg. or 65 deg., and find it the safest plan to insure strength." Mr G. Johnson (Kettering) says: "I have come to the conclusion that if a rabbitry is kept at from 50 deg. to 60 deg. it is hot enough to breed good lops, providing your hutch is small, and I am convinced that in this way you procure stronger rabbits than with larger hutches and such excessive artificial heat as 80 deg. or 90 deg., which will cause the rabbits to be poor weak things, and very small. As to breeding, I like a doe that has been brought up out of doors since the age of 7 or 8 weeks, perfect in all points, and even if with ears only 19in., it is not objectionable. Bring her into the rabbitry when old enough for breeding, and paired with as long an eared and perfectly marked buck as possible. I am satisfied that the finest rabbits are bred by crossing colours, as black buck to a yellow and white doe, or fawn to a grey and white; though to some extent you sacrifice colour, yet almost any colour may be obtained by a little care." Mr. R. Lobson (York) says: "I use no artificial heat, but keep my hutches well packed and free from cold, and at about 60 deg., give plenty of sweet hay, oats and swede turnips. As regards breeding, I like a grey and white buck to breed from, you can then have yellow and white and tortoiseshell. The orange shade of yellow so desirable you can obtain by a tortoiseshell buck and yellow doe, and a variety of colours, with judgment in the pairing."

I think little more need be said to convince all admirers of this beautiful rabbit, that the process once resorted to of "stoving," is not at all essential to insure a good specimen; but that they require more warmth during the first three or four months there can be no doubt. I by no means wish to lessen the importance attached to length of ears, providing the coveted length can be obtained by natural means, and those that are not injurious to the health of the animal.

CHAPTER XIV.

THE PATAGONIAN OR BELIAR RABBIT.

From the name of this variety it might be imagined that its original home was amongst the "Patagonian Giants" in the southern point of South America; there is, however, no record that such is a fact. Some of the finest specimens that are imported come from France and Savoy; it is impossible to say from which country the largest and best are received, though the greatest numbers come from France. Few pure-bred specimens are met with as compared with some other varieties; but as time rolls on, the Patagonian will be found in greater numbers than at present, and its merits more frequently recognised at the various exhibitions; persons are inclined, from want of knowledge, to designate any large rabbits, which are not of a decided variety, as "Patagonians," irrespective of the distinctive points which a really good specimen should possess.

In appearance this animal presents some peculiarities, in addition to its corporeal bulk, not quite in common with the other varieties; its fur, for instance, is generally of a richer and deeper colour than the ordinary grey hutch or wild rabbit, having sometimes a slightly mottled appearance, especially between the front and hind legs and upon the upper part of the body, reaching down almost as far as visible when the animal is upon the ground. The under portion is often lighter, being of a white or slightly sandy or pale yellow shade, and without the richer tints presented in the upper portions; in this particular the members of a litter will not be exactly similar, yet the more uniform they are the better. The head should be large, and broad across the eyes, and, in this respect, it cannot well be too large, and should differ from both the Belgian hare and lop; the eye should be full and large, yet giving to the whole face a happy, contented expression.

Some four or five years ago a few Patagonians were seen in this country of rather a light cream shade, but recently few of them have been found of this precise colour; when, however, in a litter of half a dozen, one of this kind occurs, if it possesses all the other requisite

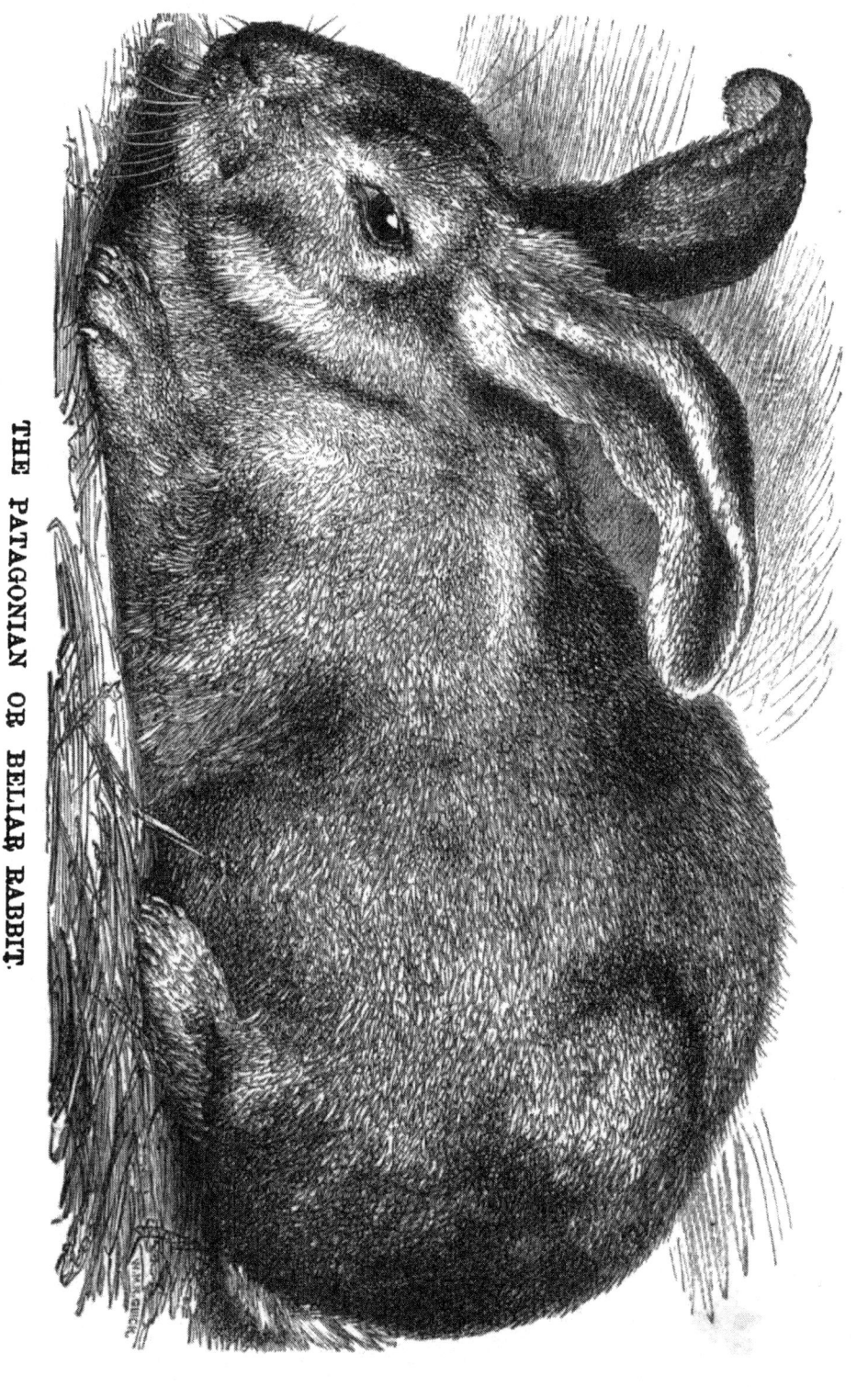

THE PATAGONIAN OR BELIAR RABBIT.

points of excellence, it should not be discarded. In the litters of recently imported animals have been found albino specimens fully equal in form, size, and all other essentials to the true shaded ones. The ears, as a rule, are broader, but less erect than those of the Belgian hare, and seem, in some instances, to have a tendency to hang down just at the tip, as if too long to remain erect. In some specimens there is a greater resemblance to the lop than desirable; yet in pairing with a short-eared one this defect may be rectified in the progeny.

In the general appearance of this noble-looking animal, there is a dignity—shall I say?—combined with a sort of happy, amiable look that ever renders it a favourite; it is by no means of a pugnacious disposition, and is exceedingly docile, rather courting than retiring from any attempt at caressing. In form it is a little different to most, if not all, other varieties; it seems to become a little wider from the neck to the loins, whilst in other kinds of rabbits the two sides are nearly parallel. Patagonians weigh from 11lb. to 14lb.; in some instances an exceptional one may be reared a little heavier, and the heavier the better, especially if the other points are good. They are not, as a rule, so prolific as some of the smaller varieties, having generally from four to seven (I have known eight) at a birth, but the smaller number is the more frequent, and it is not unusual for only two or three to be in the first litter.

As is the case always in breeding for colours and shade, a little judgment must be exercised in the pairing, in order to insure the most perfect specimens possible.

As regards the general treatment and care bestowed upon them, little need be said in addition to the directions given in reference to the Belgian hare. They will require a large hutch, with an area of 10ft. or 12ft., and 2ft. high. Many are successfully reared on the ground, in runs of any extent, and of any shape available for the purpose; a run of 20ft. or 30ft. square, would be found suitable for a dozen or twenty weaned rabbits, for two or three months, until the time for separation of the sexes; if more space than this can be afforded all the better. Young rabbits, if born in hutches, should not be placed upon the ground in damp, cold weather, but, in the summer time, they will be found to do well under wire netting, with suitable hutches to which they have access in unfavourable weather; some may be allowed to remain upon the bare ground, but others must have a space or run properly elevated and some six to twelve inches in the centre, asphalted, and provided with a small gutter beyond the wire enclosure, into which all wet and refuse may be washed. For this plan of rearing this variety a suitable position for the run or court should be selected, to insure the most genial weather at all times of the year, and to afford the greatest security during the colder months. If this protection cannot be given, the rabbits may with advantage, be removed into outside hutches for a few months during the most severe season of the year, but they must not be kept too warm, for they are very hardy, and require space and fresh air, and if the sleeping apartments are constructed in the manner spoken of when describing hutches, little other protection will be requisite during any weather. This variety is frequently crossed with the Belgian hare, to improve the size for table purposes. The Patagonian requires little to be said in its favour for culinary uses—its size bespeaks its importance and worth.

A word in conclusion as to the quantity of food consumed; in this particular this rabbit will contrast very favourably with many of the smaller varieties, when its size is taken into consideration; it will eat the same food as all the others, and is by no means dainty, nor is it difficult to rear. The skin, by reason of its large size, is valuable for many domestic purposes.

As a hint to anyone importing this variety, I suggest that the bucks be ascertained to be perfect upon arrival, for I have found more than one specimen to be totally useless for purposes of pairing. I do not assert that rabbits with this defect were intentionally supplied by the breeder or dealer, as I know that many of the larger varieties are castrated when young, in order to increase their size for the table.

CHAPTER XV.

THE SIBERIAN OR MOSCOW RABBIT.

Much may be said in favour of this very showy yet rather novel looking variety; and, though probably it may not claim the same distinctness or purity of breed as some of the other kinds reared in this country, yet its merits are sufficient to render it worthy of a place in the rabbitry. It is not so frequently seen as other better known varieties, although during the last year or two it has advanced in position, and, when exhibited, its merits have not been ignored by judges. Several countries claim the credit of being the original home of this variety, but, from all information procurable, I am inclined to the belief that it first came from the northern latitudes of Europe; in Russia and Siberia in particular it seems to have been most reared, and in all probability the first specimens were brought from there. The distinctive feature of this animal are a combination in appearance of the white Angora, with its long silky wool, and the dark extremities of the Himalayan; and the nearer approach to both, in these two all-important particulars, the more perfect and valuable the specimen. In order to insure this perfection, considerable care is requisite in pairing, for even the Himalayan itself is not always found with all the points of equal darkness. If the buck—Siberian, for instance—is found to be of the proper deep dark shade in the extremities, but not quite so long or silky in the wool as he should be, he may be paired with a doe possessing a more perfect appearance of long and silky wool, yet, to some extent, lacking the more valuable dark points. In fact, the breeding of this variety, as in all others, where two or more colours are combined, must be made a study of to insure a satisfactory result.

Foolish experimenting in crossing cannot be advised, yet anything that can be done to increase knowledge or test the truth of commonly accepted opinions, may be indulged in. To produce the Siberian rabbit from two distinct varieties, for experiment, select the darkest in points and most perfect in this particular of the Himalayan, as buck, and the longest and finest in quality of wool of the white Angora doe; and the results will be a dark tinge of the buck, but of less density, and a rather shorter coat of fur than the doe possesses in all the young ones; in fact, as may be supposed, there will be a faint imitation of both varieties, but generally that of the Himalayan will be found the more fully represented. When these are fully matured for pairing again, let each animal be mated with an animal possessing in a larger degree a development of that quality in which it seems to be deficient; and so on, with care and attention to these requirements, the fourth generation may produce almost perfect specimens. As to the size, a general average may be considered from 4lb. to 6lb., but, like all other varieties, this will depend upon the care bestowed in feeding, &c.; also the parentage and number brought up by the doe. They sometimes reach 7½lb. and 8lb., but, when so large, it will be generally found that in the most desirable points they are not so perfect as those of a medium size. They are gentle in disposition, and are moderately prolific, when compared with others of corresponding size, from five to eight at a birth being the usual average. Little deviation in their general management, feeding, &c., need be made from that of the Angora or Himalayan; they are equally hardy, and, in a warm sheltered position, will thrive in outside hutches, with the addition of a little extra protection during the severe and inclement weather. To secure the finer silky quality of the fur, it will be found an advantage to allow them to remain out during the summer months only, but they by no means require the higher temperature so essential to the satisfactory development of the lop; if the rabbitry generally is well ventilated, and at moderate temperature they may be permanently kept there with success. On the continent, particularly in France, this variety is much prized by all grades of fanciers, and is more common than with us.

ADVERTISEMENTS.

BOOKS PUBLISHED BY HORACE COX,
AT 346, STRAND, W.C.

THE IDSTONE PAPERS.—A Series of Articles and Desultory Observations on Sport and Things in General, written originally for *The Field* newspaper. By "IDSTONE," of *The Field*. Large post 8vo., price 7s. 6d.

THE DIAMOND DIGGINGS of SOUTH AFRICA.—A Personal and Practical Account. By "SARCELLE," of *The Field*. With a Brief Notice of the New Gold Fields. With Map, large post 8vo., price 6s.

ROUND the TABLE; or, Notes on Cookery and Plain Recipes, with a Selection of Bills of Fare. By "The G. C." All its recipes have been tested by experience, and are so given as to be intelligible of themselves, the object being not so much to provide a volume of reference for a professed cook as to explain how, with ordinary resources, an artistic dinner can be produced. Post 8vo., price 6s.

SECOND EDITION of the DOGS of the BRITISH ISLANDS. Edited by "STONEHENGE." Greatly enlarged (including new Parts on "Kennel Management of Dogs," and "Judging at Dog Shows and Field Trials"). 4to., gilt edges, toned paper, price 10s. 6d.

UNASKED ADVICE: a Series of Articles on Horses and Hunting, interesting to Ladies as well as Gentlemen. By "IMPECUNIOSUS," who says in his preface "they recommend nothing which has not been personally tried and found to answer." Post 8vo., with 13 Engravings printed on toned paper, price 7s. 6d.

THE RURAL ALMANAC and SPORTSMAN'S ILLUSTRATED CALENDAR for 1874. Price 1s.; by post, 1s. 2d.

THE ANGLER'S DIARY, wherein the Angler can Register his Take of Fish throughout the Year. An extensive List of Fishing Stations throughout the World is added. Post 8vo., price 1s. 6d.; post free, 1s. 8d. In cloth, 2s.; post free, 2s. 2d.

THE SHOOTER'S DIARY contains Forms for Registering Game killed during the Year, either by a Single Gun or by a Party, or off the whole Estate. A List of Shooting Stations throughout the World is also given. Post 4to., price 1s. 6d.; post free, 2d. extra.

FACTS and USEFUL HINTS relating to FISHING and SHOOTING, Illustrated; being a Collection of Information and Recipes of the greatest utility to the general Sportsman, to which is added a Series of Recipes on the Management of Dogs in Health and Disease. Third Edition, enlarged and revised. Large post 8vo., price 7s. 6d. cloth.

THE COUNTRY HOUSE; a Collection of Useful Information and Recipes of the greatest utility to the housekeeper generally. Illustrated. Second Edition, enlarged and revised. Large post 8vo., price 5s. cloth.

THE FARM: being Part I. of the Second Edition of the FARM, GARDEN, STABLE, and AVIARY. Valuable to country gentlemen, farmers, &c. Large post 8vo., price 5s.

THE GARDEN: being Part II. of the Second Edition of the FARM, GARDEN, STABLE, and AVIARY. Large post 8vo., price 5s.

THE STABLE: being Part III. of the Second Edition of the FARM, GARDEN, STABLE, and AVIARY. Large post 8vo., price 5s.

THE COUNTRY
A JOURNAL OF RURAL PURSUITS.

PUBLISHED EVERY THURSDAY, PRICE TWOPENCE.

CONTENTS.

Fishing and Shooting.—Current Events noted; Articles and Letters from various Correspondents on the many questions embraced by these sports.

Kennel and Stable.—Articles on Dogs and Horses; Reports of Shows, &c.

Natural Science.—Articles and Letters on Entomology, Botany, Zoology, &c.

Far and Near.—Emigration fully treated; Travels in all Countries; Epitome of recent Geographical discoveries and doings.

Farm and Garden.—Reports of Meetings of Agricultural and Horticultural Societies; Articles interesting to the Farmer, professional and amateur; Gardening in all its branches; Cultural directions for various flowers and fruits, both out of doors and under glass.

Poultry and Rabbits.—Articles on Poultry, Pigeons, and Rabbits; full reports of Shows.

Aviary and Apiary.—Articles and Notes on Cage Birds and Bee Keeping.

REPORTS OF ALL IMPORTANT EVENTS IN
RACING, ATHLETICS, CRICKET, ROWING, ARCHERY, YACHTING, CROQUET, GOLF, AND OTHER SPORTS.

Quarterly Subscription, prepaid, 2s. 8d.

OFFICE: 32, WELLINGTON STREET, STRAND, LONDON, W.C.

CPSIA information can be obtained
at www.ICGtesting.com
Printed in the USA
BVOW07s0958210316
441131BV00004B/12/P